Assignment

Whisper

Assignment Whisper

Mary Gant Bell
2009

ISBN: 978-0-578-00795-3

*Dedicated to my husband
who has always
encouraged me to whisper*

*With special thanks to
the numerous others who
contributed to this devotional,
especially Carina,
my dear friend and editor*

Welcome

Welcome to *Assignment Whisper*. I am excited that you decided to purchase this devotional and hope that you enjoy learning to "whisper" to others. I pray that by the end of the year, you will discover a deep-seeded joy from touching the lives of others in unique and unusual ways.

Countless times people have told me that they want to do *something*, but they stumble with that first step. Use this book as a way to stimulate your creativity. You might decide to try each suggestion as presented. If you find one that speaks to your talents, remain with that all year long. Others pray over each suggestion. All of those are appropriate uses for this devotional.

Please do not feel overwhelmed by the prospect of whispering. This devotional is not intended to push you past your limit. I encourage you to go beyond the limit of your comfort zone, but I do not recommend that you go beyond your financial means. You determine those limits.

Although I write from a Christian perspective, I believe that the ideas and suggestions of this devotional apply to any faith. I have studied other religions and have had the pleasure of knowing people of different spiritual convictions. Meeting someone without a kind heart and willingness to help others regardless of their spiritual position is extremely rare. If you are not Christian, you may need to modify some of my suggestions.

Each page includes space to make notes, record contact phone numbers, etc. When you find an activity that touches your heart, document any information that will help you later. I also encourage you to document the reactions of the recipients of your kindness. Record your impact on the world and rejoice in the opportunity to touch others.

The New International Version of the Bible was used for the quotes in this devotional. I encourage you to visit www.blueletterbible.org to read each verse in context. This website also provides several Bible translations to facilitate reading these verses in the version of your choice. Word definitions come from the lexicon on this website as well.

Stories and jokes included in this devotional strive to stimulate your creativity and challenge your perspective. Uncovering original authors proved challenging, however. Credit is sited when possible.

Please allow me to share your whispering experiences on my website:

www.assignmentwhisper.com

Read stories from fellow whisperers about how their volunteering has impacted the world. Become involved with other projects and events organized by *Assignment Whisper*. I look forward to hearing from you and sharing your stories with others.

Now it is time to open your hearts, turn the page, and begin the journey.

Themes

January	New Beginnings
February	Love
March	Purpose
April	Commitment
May	Beauty
June	Prayer and Communication
July	Nation
August	Forgiveness
September	Rest
October	Appreciation
November	Thankfulness
December	Gifts

* *Assignment Whisper* *

January 1

Some people enjoy being in the spotlight, soaking up the attention of the masses. Others find comfort with one-on-one situations. Not all of us are called to be public figures or household names.

Assignment Whisper is based on I Kings 19: 11-12, which states:

The Lord said, "Go out and stand on the mountain in the presence of the Lord, for the Lord is about to pass by." Then a great and powerful wind tore the mountains apart and shattered the rocks before the Lord, but the Lord was not in the wind. After the wind there was an earthquake, but the Lord was not in the earthquake. After the earthquake came a fire, but the Lord was not in the fire. And after the fire came a gentle whisper.

Today, focus on the strength of God's presence in the small things as well as the large. His company can be felt just as powerfully in an earthquake as in a whisper. Whatever you do today, become aware of God's presence in your life. Listen to the way that He whispers to you personally.

The presence of the Lord is about to pass by. Take notice!

January 2

God is omnipresent. That means He remains everywhere at all times. As we read in I Kings yesterday, He was equally present in the wind, earthquake, fire, and whisper. Notice Him in your kitchen, in your cubical at work, in your car during traffic, in your laughter at a joke, and by your side during crisis. He resides with you always. You are in His presence no matter where you are, what you do, or how you feel.

Yesterday, you focused on recognizing God's presence in your own life. Resolve now to be present in the lives of others. Make each person you meet feel that they are important and appreciated. Help them to see that they are also in the presence of God and how valuable they are in God's eyes. Resolve to make everyone – friends and strangers alike – feel valuable.

Review these verses that show God's presence:

If I go up to the heavens, you are there; if I make my bed in the depths, you are there.
Psalm 139:8

"Am I only a God nearby," declares the Lord, "and not a God far away? Can anyone hide in secret places so that I cannot see him?" declares the Lord. "Do not I fill heaven and earth?" declares the Lord.
Jeremiah 23:23-24

But will God really dwell on earth? The heavens, even the highest heaven, cannot contain you. How much less this temple I have built!
Kings 8:27

* *Assignment Whisper* *

January 3

Before spreading out into the world, begin impacting others in your own home. Today focus on your spouse.

Thank your spouse for loving you. This does not mean to simply tell your spouse that you love him or her. Strive to ensure that your spouse realizes how much it means to you that he or she loves you – warts and all.

The heart of her husband safely trusts her; so he will have no lack of gain. She does him good and not evil all the days of her life.
Proverbs 31:11-12

However, each one of you also must love his wife as he loves himself, and the wife must respect her husband.
Ephesians 5:33

If you are not married or in a relationship, select another family member or close friend. Let that important person in your life know that you appreciate his or her love for you. Tell this special person how his or her love makes you a better person.

For some of you, this assignment is effortless and comes naturally. Some of you are thinking that saying it aloud wastes a breath. Surely your spouse already knows. Regardless, say it anyway.

* *Assignment Whisper* *

January 4

Today's whispering assignment builds on yesterday's focus. Tell your children how much the love of each of them means to you. Even if today turns into one of those days that make you question your sanity as a parent, take each of your children aside and tell him or her individually how much you value each of them. Yes, that even applies to the teenagers who do not want to be caught dead with parents. Tell that child, too.

If you do not have children, use this day to share your thoughts with a sibling or close relative. Let your family members know how much their love and support means to you.

Some people appear to shun love. That is a fact of life. Children go through stages that make the enjoyable times few and far between. Remember that even the most difficult children still have cheerful days. Recall just one of those pleasant times, and tell your child that you have happy memories with him or her. Together you can remember today as another day for the memory book.

* *Assignment Whisper* *

January 5

Smile at five strangers today. Make it a genuine smile to brighten their day. Be bold and add a "Good day" or "Hello" to your smile.

Some of you live in large cities; others live in rural areas. Most people can say that they see some of the same folks every day. This might be your neighbor, your letter carrier, or your children's teachers. Other people glimpse multitudes of strangers each day. If you live in a place like New York City, you might feel overwhelmed with the number of bodies around you.

I recently visited Washington DC. Riding the subway and visiting national monuments with throngs of tourists put me in contact with more people in one week than I normally see in a year. By the end of the week, I noticed myself progressively tuning out the those around me. The volume of faces became overwhelming.

Make a decision to remember that all of these individuals are people just like you. They all have hopes, dreams, worries, and demands on their time. They could each feel as overwhelmed as I did on the Metro.

We all have reasons for shutting out the world. Today the goal is to make people feel as if they were noticed. You might be the only individual in their day that actually looked at them and acknowledged them. So put on your smile and impact the world!

* Assignment Whisper *

January 6

Take a treat to your grocery store check-out clerk today.

When I was in high school, I worked at the local grocery store as a check-out clerk. Two ladies came to the store every week to do their shopping together. When they got their carts, they also picked up a bag of potato chips. They snacked on chips while shopping as though it was a grand adventure.

Their cheerfulness was contagious. The staff came alive the minute they entered the store. The anticipation of their arrival at the checkout was palpable despite the fact that none of us saw them as they shopped. Before unloading their cart, they included a second bag of chips to share with the employees. They let us join in their adventure, and it was fun every time.

Buy a treat for your checkout person today at whatever store you frequent. It is sure to brighten their day.

January 7

Volunteer at the Special Olympics in your area. If you do not have one, consider organizing it.
Visit this website to help you get started: www.specialolympics.org.
If you are unable to participate for some reason, pray for those who participate and their families. If finances allow, donate cash on their website.
According to www.specialolympics.org:
"Special Olympics is an international nonprofit organization dedicated to empowering individuals with intellectual disabilities to become physically fit, productive and respected members of society through sports training and competition. Special Olympics offers children and adults with intellectual disabilities year-round training and competition in 30 Olympic-type summer and winter sports.
Children and adults with intellectual disabilities who participate in Special Olympics develop improved physical fitness and motor skills, greater self-confidence and a more positive self-image. They grow mentally, socially and spiritually and, through their activities, exhibit boundless courage and enthusiasm, enjoy the rewards of friendship and ultimately discover not only new abilities and talents but 'their voices' as well.."

* *Assignment Whisper* *

January 8

<u>Volunteering Fact</u>
According to www.worldvolunteerweb.org:
"15.5 million youths between the ages of 12 and 18 contributed more than 1.3 billion hours of service during 2004."

If you have children in this age category, model the volunteering spirit to them. Find opportunities that involve your children as much as possible. Help the youth, the future of our nation, find their calling. Assist them in creating a life pattern of helping others.

Remember that other children are watching your children. By encouraging these activities with your own children, their friends observe it, too. Whenever possible, encourage your kids to invite their friends to join your volunteering adventures. Include their parents as well.

Who are the children you will influence?

* *Assignment Whisper* *

January 9

<u>Book Recommendation</u>
Improving Your Serve: The Art of Unselfish Living
by Charles R. Swindoll
Any book by Charles Swindoll captivates me. To learn how to ignite your serving spirit, this book is a must read.

Mr. Swindoll reminds us that:
"No selfless act is so small, no good deed so insignificant, that God cannot see and approve. ....
It is, in fact, the very substance and context of the Great Commission which tells us that we are to transmit the gospel to others, not only in our confession of Christ but by displaying in our lives a daily example of Christ's love." (page 211)

This book will illuminate just what it means to serve others in a selfless fashion.

Note here what impacted you the most as you read this book.

* *Assignment Whisper* *

January 10

Take a treat to your bank tellers today. Tell them how much you appreciate their service.

So often when we go to the bank, financial matters consume our brain power. Even in the drive-through lanes, our attention shifts to other things while these nameless people processes our transactions. They routinely tell us their names as they ask how they can assist. Yet how many times do we actually remember their names? Would you recognize your bank teller in the grocery store line?

Here are some ideas to brighten their day:

- ❖ Take cookies.
- ❖ Write thank you notes. Deliver them in person or put them in the mail.
- ❖ Cut a small bouquet of fresh flowers from your garden.
- ❖ Bring your children to sing a cheerful song.
- ❖ Donate hand lotion; counting money all day can dry skin.
- ❖ Order pizza delivered for their lunch.
- ❖ Note your own ideas here.

* *Assignment Whisper* *

January 11

Donate food to the local animal shelter today. The organization can always use donations of food, toys, blankets, and hand sanitizers as well as your time and energy.

If animals are not your passion, ask for ways that you can contribute without having contact with the animals. Perhaps the association needs assistance writing donation letters or restocking shelves. Be creative.

There are animal rights agencies that also use volunteers. Here are some options to investigate:
- ❖ Society for Prevention of Cruelty to Animals www.spca.com
- ❖ The Human Society www.hsus.org
- ❖ Green Peace www.greenpeace.org
- ❖ Animal Rights Activists Group
- ❖ Speak up 4 Animal Rights www.geocities.com/jillserena/Speakup4Ani malRights.html

* *Assignment Whisper* *

January 12

"I've never been one of physical exercise," she said, "but what God does with our faith must be something like workouts. He sees to it that our faith gets pushed and pulled, stretched and pounded, taken to its limits so its limits can expand."

He liked that - taken to its limits so its limits can expand. Yes!

"If it doesn't get exercised," she said thoughtfully, "it becomes like a weak muscle that fails us when we need it."

He felt himself smiling foolishly, though his question was serious. "Would you agree that we must be willing to thank God for every trial of our faith, no matter how severe, for the greater strength it produces?"

"I'm perfectly willing to say it, but I'm continually unable to do it."

"There's the rub!"

At Home in Mitford
by Jan Karon
Page 158

What trials in your life strengthened and shaped you into the person you are today? How can you use these experiences to whisper to others?

* *Assignment Whisper* *

January 13

Take flowers to the health club receptionist today.

January is traditionally the month for people to rededicate themselves to exercising. New Year's Resolutions burst forth as thick as mosquitoes after a rainstorm. Whether you have been a member of a health club for years or recently joined through the January specials, remember the receptionist today.

The receptionist is one of those invisible people. No one really gives them credit for doing anything more than smiling and greeting people. Yet their duties involve so much more than what you see. They ensure the smooth and efficient operations throughout the gym.

If you do not believe this, just think about a place where you perceived that the receptionist was dreadful. Receptionists are like drivers - no one notices their driving unless it is awful. People ignore the receptionist except when they are inefficient. An employee without job duties cannot be lame. Therefore, they must do something.

Take the time today to acknowledge what a great job the receptionist does. Let the receptionist staff know that you appreciate their contribution to the operation of the health club.

* *Assignment Whisper* *

January 14

On my way home one day, I stopped to watch a Little League baseball game that was being played in a park near my home. As I sat down behind the bench on the first-base line, I asked one of the boys what the score was.

"We're behind 14 to nothing," he answered with a smile.

"Really," I said. "I have to say you don't look very discouraged."

"Discouraged?" the boy asked with a puzzled look on his face. "Why should we be discouraged? We haven't been up to bat yet."

What distorted your perception today?
Have you left the game before swinging the bat?

January 15

Do something for your neighbor today. Choose a neighbor whom you may not like. Create an opportunity to talk when there are no pressing issues demanding resolution.

Most everyone suffers through a difficult neighbor at some point. After reading the story on perspective yesterday, consider there might be a different point of view to your neighbor. Plan to meet this person with an open mind, an open heart, and no agenda.

Here are some ideas:

- ❖ Take cookies.
- ❖ Volunteer to walk your neighbor's dog.
- ❖ Discuss gardening and compliment his or her skill in growing lovely things.
- ❖ Take a bouquet of flowers from your own garden.
- ❖ Volunteer to do a difficult chore.
- ❖ Offer to pick up something at the store.
- ❖ Take a bird feeder or bird seed.
- ❖ Note your ideas here.

* *Assignment Whisper* *

January 16

"If busyness is an emotional complex, then it's likely that when we are busiest, we are doing least. We can be extremely active without being busy, and busy without accomplishing anything. We may be feverishly engaged in some task and yet not truly focused on the matter at hand. The job may be merely a means to accomplish some other goal: to make money, to impress, or to prove oneself to another. Our busyness may be a way to avoid difficult emotions and thoughts, or we may simply believe that it's important never to waste time."

Thomas Moore

Has this devotional made you busy or active? How do you think you have changed in the past fifteen days? What modifications are necessary as you move forward through this book?

* *Assignment Whisper* *

January 17

Help someone get organized today – even if it is you!

Sometimes cleaning one particular area in your home can impact organization throughout the house. Most everyone designates one spot where things pile and remain. Tackle your pile today and start the process of organization. You might need to plan a garage sale, but you will definitely become more structured by getting the clutter out of your life.

Are there any emotional or spiritual things that are cluttering your heart? Take an emotional inventory to evaluate the need to be purged your soul as well as your closets.

Do you have a mental "to do" list of tasks that refuse to budge? List these tasks on paper. Organize them in a way that facilitates their completion. Delegate what you can. Dedicate 15-30 minutes a day or a week to what remains on the list. Consider hiring a neighborhood teenager to help.

List here the things that you were able to cross off the list today. Begin the new year with a shorter, more manageable list.

January 18

Donate a lap quilt to a nursing home today.

Nursing homes are full of fascinating people with interesting life stories. Spend some time talking to them today. If you reflect on how much the world has changed just in your own lifetime, consider how much it has changed in the life span of someone twice your age. How did they live without being constantly connected by cell phones!?!

Many nursing home residents suffer from loneliness. Even a brief visit of 30 minutes could make a world of difference in someone's day. If you are uncomfortable talking to strangers, walk the hallways sharing smiles with everyone you pass. Linger at every doorway is not required. Make eye contact and smile.

If regular visits ease into your calendar, ask the staff what activities the residents enjoy. Perhaps you could start a scrapbooking club or a monthly bingo night. Take your karaoke machine and see what happens. There are endless possibilities.

If you do not know anyone in a nursing home, look in your phone book or call your doctor's office.

Jot down what you learned from your visit.

* *Assignment Whisper* *

January 19

Adopt a missionary today.

Write letters and pray for that person and their family. It may seem as if missionaries have support and appreciation, but this is not always the case.

Writing to a missionary is also a great way to teach your children about geography and other cultures. If you have school aged children, make this a literary project and read about the country.

If your church lacks information about missionaries, visit: www.missionary-blogs.com

January 20

<u>The Cab Ride</u>
by Ken Nerburn
from his book, *Make Me an Instrument of Your Peace: Living in the Spirit of the Prayer of St. Francis*

Twenty years ago, I drove a cab for a living. When I arrived at 2:30 a. m., the building was dark except for a single light in a ground floor window. Under these circumstances, many drivers would just honk once or twice, wait a minute, and then drive away.

But I had seen too many impoverished people who depended on taxis as their only means of transportation. Unless a situation smelled of danger, I always went to the door. This passenger might be someone who needs my assistance, I reasoned to myself.

So I walked to the door and knocked.

"Just a minute", answered a frail, elderly voice. I could hear something being dragged across the floor.

After a long pause, the door opened. A small woman in her 80's stood before me. She was wearing a print dress and a pillbox hat with a veil pinned on it, like somebody out of a 1940s movie. By her side was a small nylon suitcase. The apartment looked as if no one had lived in it for years. All the furniture was covered with sheets. There were no clocks on the walls, no knickknacks or utensils on the counters. In the corner was a cardboard box filled with photos and glassware.

"Would you carry my bag out to the car?" she said.

* _Assignment Whisper_ *

I took the suitcase to the cab, and then returned to assist the woman. She took my arm and we walked slowly toward the curb. She kept thanking me for my kindness.

"It's nothing", I told her. "I just try to treat my passengers the way I would want my mother treated."

"Oh, you're such a good boy", she said.

When we got in the cab, she gave me an address, and then asked, "Could you drive through downtown?"

"It's not the shortest way," I answered quickly.

"Oh, I don't mind," she said. "I'm in no hurry. I'm on my way to a hospice".

I looked in the rear-view mirror. Her eyes were glistening. "I don't have any family left," she continued. "The doctor says I don't have very long."

I quietly reached over and shut off the meter. "What route would you like me to take?" I asked. For the next two hours, we drove through the city. She showed me the building where she had once worked as an elevator operator. We drove through the neighborhood where she and her husband had lived when they were newlyweds. She had me pull up in front of a furniture warehouse that had once been a ballroom where she had gone dancing as a girl. Sometimes she'd ask me to slow in front of a particular building or corner and would sit staring into the darkness, saying nothing.

As the first hint of sun was creasing the horizon, she suddenly said, "I'm tired. Let's go now."

We drove in silence to the address she had given me. It was a low building, like a small convalescent home, with a driveway that passed under a portico. Two orderlies came out to the cab as soon as we pulled up. They were solicitous and intent, watching her every move. They must have been expecting her.

* _Assignment Whisper_ *

I opened the trunk and took the small suitcase to the door. The woman was already seated in a wheelchair.

"How much do I owe you?" she asked, reaching into her purse.

"Nothing," I said.

"You have to make a living," she answered.

"There are other passengers," I responded. Almost without thinking, I bent and gave her a hug.

She held onto me tightly. "You gave an old woman a little moment of joy," she said. "Thank you."

I squeezed her hand, and then walked into the dim morning light. Behind me, a door shut. It was the sound of the closing of a life. I didn't pick up any more passengers that shift. I drove aimlessly lost in thought. For the rest of that day, I could hardly talk.

What if that woman had gotten an angry driver, or one who was impatient to end his shift? What if I had refused to take the run, or had honked once, then driven away? On a quick review, I don't think that I have done anything more important in my life.

We're conditioned to think that our lives revolve around great moments. But great moments often catch us unaware-beautifully wrapped in what others may consider a small one. People may not remember exactly what you did or what you said, but they will always remember how you made them feel.

What feelings did you invoke in others today?

* *Assignment Whisper* *

January 21

"People become really quite remarkable when they start thinking that they can do things. When they believe in themselves they have the first secret of success."

Norman Vincent Peale

Express your confidence and faith in someone today. Share your thoughts with that person.

Tell yourself that you believe in you. You are truly remarkable. Even if no one ever says those words aloud to you, it remains true. You are remarkable, unique, and amazing. You deserve love, respect, and admiration. Believing those things about yourself will unlock forgotten energy into your life.

Remember from childhood how easily the belief in Santa rooted in your heart? Even as an adult we refuse to doubt certain ideas. The sun rises in the east. Stars illuminate the night sky. The grocery store sells milk despite their lack of cows. We accept numerous things without proof or depth of understanding.

Yet when it comes to something as important as ourselves, we complicate the matter. We try to add conditions or comparisons. We doubt our own worth and value to others. Today, remind yourself how important you are. After repeating these reminders to yourself, express to others how much you believe in them, too.

January 22

Read a book on tape and donate it to Lighthouse for the Blind.

The Lighthouse for the Blind offers a variety of services to the visually impaired. Reading book, newspapers, or magazines on tape provides a valuable resource and one that can be done from home.

The Lighthouse also needs people to be home visitors, assisting with daily household chores. What would you do if you could not read your mail or write checks to pay the bills? Helping with the small things can make a huge difference to someone whose sight is impaired.

The Lighthouse for the Blind also works in schools, community centers, and churches. If you are uncomfortable working directly with blind people, perhaps you could help coordinate schedules and arrange tables and chairs. Annual fundraisers always need organized people as well.

Visit their website www.lighthouse.org to locate a facility close to you.

January 23

Send a card to your best friend, even if he or she lives next door or talks to you daily.

Remember when the mailbox contained more than bills? Remember how much fun it was to receive a personal letter in the mail? Before emails and the depersonalization of communication, a trip to the mailbox included a visit from a friend.

Find some pretty note cards and start writing. It isn't so hard once you get going on the idea. Write to someone detached from computer equipment. Mail a note card to your best friend, even thought you talk to him or her each day.

In the fall of 2008, we were without electricity for twelve days because of Hurricane Ike. It was shocking just how disconcerting it felt to be disconnected from the internet for that long. I had visions of my computer crashing because of the volume of unread emails. I was cut off from so many friends without the internet or telephones.

Amazingly enough, the mail only stopped for two days following Hurricane Ike. Yet not so surprisingly, no one thought to write me an old-fashioned letter. It would have been so wonderful to receive a letter from a friend in that electronic void.

Do not wait for a natural disaster to make someone smile. Write a letter today and put it in the mail. I promise the mailbox will not eat your hand.

January 24

Do something for the letter carrier today.

Remember those letters you mailed yesterday? Well, someone delivered them for you. Thank your letter carrier for a job well done. Let that person know that you appreciate what he or she does even if you think computers rule the world of communication. Break the monotony of the work day with something distinctive.

Some ideas of things to do are:

❖ Put a candy bar in your mailbox for him/her.

❖ Ask for a pick up at your house so that you can thank him or her in person.

❖ Prepare a cup of hot cocoa.

❖ Knit a colorful scarf.

❖ Buy a pair of warm gloves.

❖ Pray for him or her.

❖ Make origami animals out of circulars you receive in the mail.

❖ Put cheerful stickers on your outgoing mail.

❖ Note your ideas here.

January 25

Say something pleasant and uplifting to your boss today.

This might be a hard task for some of you, but do it anyway. If your boss is a difficult person, perhaps some kindness will improve his or her disposition. If a wonderful boss greets you each work day, he or she still deserves to hear your encouraging words.

If you have never been a manager or supervisor, do not underestimate the difficulties inherent to that position. Even managers answer to a superior. Your boss is often just a middle man, taking heat from both sides of the hierarchy. Remember that despite the times that you disagree with company decision, you are all just people. Your manager or supervisor possesses strengths and weaknesses, struggles and pains, just like you do. Understanding how decisions are made is not a requirement to showing respect.

If you do not work outside the home, your spouse is your boss. Encourage your spouse today. If you are your own boss, look in the mirror and say something inspiring to yourself about yourself. Remember to smile when you say it.

January 26

Today is "look behind you" day. How many times a day are there people physically behind us that we fail to acknowledge? Take some time today to notice these folks in some way.

- ❖ Pay the toll of the car behind you.
- ❖ Pay for the coffee of the person behind you at the local coffee shop.
- ❖ Buy a bottle of water for the person behind you at the gas station.
- ❖ Pay a little extra to the dry cleaner if there is someone behind you in line.
- ❖ If the person behind you at the library circular desk has fines for overdue books, make a donation.
- ❖ Bag the groceries of the person behind you in the grocery store line.
- ❖ Buy a package of gum for the person boarding the airplane behind you if you are traveling.
- ❖ Note your ideas here.

Notice the people behind you today. Who did you see? Start the new year with the habit of noticing the people behind you.

* *Assignment Whisper* *

January 27

Teach your children a new responsibility today.

Regardless of the age of your child or children, you can always ask them to do more around the house. Make it a game if it helps. Sing a song. If your children are grown and independent, suggest that they take on a new task around their own home. Encourage your children to relieve someone else of a chore burden.

Try to select a chore for each child that is something that will benefit the entire family. Do not delegate your least favorite chore. Kids are smart; they will pick up on that in a heartbeat! The idea is to teach them responsibility, not make them feel as if you are dumping your "nasties" on them.

Assigning chores to your children will make them feel like a valued part of the family. It will also help them to realize that you trust them with the task. By treating them like children, they will continue to act like children. Raise the bar today. Give them a chore that demonstrates that you see them as a accountable person and respected member of the family.

Some parents do not believe in giving their children chores. Most parents want their children to have a better life than they did. However, chores are not punishment. Responsibility is not the same as restrictions. Make your child an active part of their own life. They will thank you for it when they are grown (or their spouse will!)

* *Assignment Whisper* *

January 28

"For I know the plans I have for you," declares the Lord, "plans to prosper you and not to harm you, plans to give you hope and a future."

Jeremiah 29:11

What does "prosper" mean to you? Does it mean financial success? Does it imply a particular job title? Does it require a new pair of shoes?

Spend some time defining this term as it relates to your own life. It is very difficult to achieve something that you cannot define. Make your own version of prosperity clear. Then share your ideas with God through prayer.

Consider how others in your life would define "prosper" for themselves. Think of some ways that you can help them achieve their prosperity. Does it require simple encouragement or something more? Does your spouse's prosperity require some sacrifice on your part? Is it something you are able and willing to do for your other half?

Seriously consider what "prosperity" means from the eyes of your children. Depending on their ages, their definitions might seem silly to you. However, it is important to remember that from their perspective, their view is just as significant as your goals are to you. As much as possible, try to help them define and achieve their own prosperity. Teach them from an early age to dream and work to accomplish their dreams.

Evaluate whether your definition of prosperity requires changing habits and beginning the new year with modified behaviors in your life.

* *Assignment Whisper* *

January 29

Take flowers to your church's secretary today.

The church secretary is the personification of "servant leadership" in my humble opinion. They are often forgotten and yet indispensible to the operation of any church. Now that the Christmas season has passed, the decorations are stored, and the church office has a lull in activities before Easter, show the church's secretary how much you appreciate all that he or she contributes to the church. So much of what happens behind the scenes is organized by these people. Someone had to make sure that everything ran smoothly during the holidays. Guess who that was!

If you do not belong to a church, pick the church that you drive past regularly. If you are not religious in any fashion, do it anyway. The church secretary is a person, just like you. We all like to be appreciated and remembered.

Besides, flowers in January are just plain fun!

* *Assignment Whisper* *

January 30

Cookies dominate my agenda today. Everyone loves cookies. Most people I know will break their diets for a nibble or two. Almost everyone has a favorite. As soon as the cookie try slides into the oven, their aroma brightens our day.

Host a cookie party to donate the cookies. Pick a time now and tell your friends to reserve the date. Everyone brings a box or two of cookies to donate. Once you have gathered all of your donated boxes of cookies, decide where you will donate them.

My personal favorite donation idea continues to be sending cookies to soldiers in a combat zone. Nothing says home like a box of cookies. During your party, write letters to the soldiers telling them how much you appreciate their service.

Assisted living centers would also appreciate cookies. Check with the staff, however, before doing this as some residents will have dietary restrictions. These people would also appreciate notes and letters. Deliver these on a day when you can stay and play a game of Bingo as you share the cookies.

Grease the cookie sheet and sift the flower. Enjoy the pleasure of sharing home-baked love after you sample a cookie or two!

* *Assignment Whisper* *

January 31

Let us not become weary in doing good, for at the proper time we will reap a harvest if we do not give up.

Galatians 6:9

Does the first month of ideas have you weary? Are you beginning to wonder why you bought this book?

I encourage you to persevere. If exhaustion overwhelms you, continue to pray over the ideas and people suggested each day. There is no time limit for completion. Remember that this devotional is not intended to be more than you can handle. Push yourself, but do not break. Remember that you are not alone. Strength is just a prayer away.

My hope is that you are feeling energized and revitalized by helping others. A giving heart provides rest and comfort in ways we cannot anticipate. Spend some time today evaluating how you have changed in the last month with regard to helping others. Note what comes to mind here.

* *Assignment Whisper* *

February 1

God is called many different names in the Bible. It is easy to find books written about this topic. When reading the meanings of the names used for God, they all point to one thing – how much He loves us. This is my favorite list of God's love. To the best of my knowledge, the author is unknown.

In Genesis, HE IS the Creator God.
In Exodus, HE IS the Redeemer.
In Leviticus, HE IS your Sanctifier.
In Numbers, HE IS your Guide.
In Deuteronomy, HE IS your Teacher.
In Joshua, HE IS the Mighty Conqueror.
In Judges, He gives victory over enemies.
In Ruth, HE IS your Kinsman, your Lover, and your Redeemer.
In 1st Samuel, HE IS the Root of Jesse.
In 2nd Samuel, HE IS the Son of David.
In 1st and 2nd Kings, HE IS King of Kings and Lord of Lords.
In 1st and 2nd Chronicles, HE IS your Intercessor and High Priest.
In Ezra, HE IS your temple, your house of worship.
In Nehemiah, HE IS your mighty wall, protecting you from your enemies.
In Esther, He stands in the gap to deliver you from your enemies.
In Job, HE IS the Arbitrator who not only understands your struggles, but has the power to do something about them.
In Psalms, HE IS your Song - and your reason to sing.
In Proverbs, HE IS your wisdom, helping you make sense of life and live it successfully.

In Ecclesiastes, HE IS your purpose, delivering you from vanity.

In the Song of Solomon, HE IS your Lover, your Rose of Sharon.

In Isaiah, HE IS the Mighty Counselor, the Prince of Peace, the Everlasting Father, and more. In short, He's everything you need.

In Jeremiah, HE IS your Balm in Gilead, the soothing salve for your sin-sick soul.

In Lamentations, HE IS the ever-faithful One upon Whom you can depend.

In Ezekiel, HE IS your Wheel in the middle of a wheel -- the One who assures that dry, dead bones will come alive again.

In Daniel, HE IS the Ancient of Days, the everlasting God who never runs out of time.

In Hosea, HE IS your Faithful Lover, always beckoning you to come back - when you have abandoned Him.

In Joel, HE IS your Refuge, keeping you safe in times of trouble.

In Amos, HE IS the Husbandman, the One you can depend on to stay by your side.

In Obadiah, HE IS Lord of the Kingdom.

In Jonah, HE IS your Salvation, bringing you back within His will.

In Micah, HE IS Judge of the nation.

In Nahum, HE IS the jealous God.

In Habakkuk, HE IS the Holy One.

In Zephaniah, HE IS the Witness.

In Haggai, He overthrows the enemies.

In Zechariah, HE IS Lord of Hosts.

In Malachi, HE IS Merciful.

In Matthew, HE IS King of the Jews.

In Mark, HE IS the Servant.

In Luke, HE IS the Son of Man, feeling what you feel.
In John, HE IS the Son of God.
In Acts, HE IS the Savior of the world.
In Romans, HE IS the righteousness of God.
In 1st Corinthians, HE IS the Rock that followed Israel.
In 2nd Corinthians, HE IS the Triumphant One, living victory.
In Galatians, HE IS your liberty; He sets you free.
In Ephesians, HE IS Head of the Church.
In Philippians, HE IS your joy.
In Colossians, HE IS your completeness.
In 1st and 2nd Thessalonians, HE IS your hope.
In 1st Timothy, HE IS your faith.
In 2nd Timothy, HE IS your stability.
In Philemon, HE IS your Benefactor.
In Titus, HE IS truth.
In Hebrews, HE IS your perfection.
In James, HE IS the Power behind your faith.
In 1st Peter, HE IS your example.
In 2nd Peter, HE IS your purity.
In 1st John, HE IS your life.
In 2nd John, HE IS your pattern.
In 3rd John, HE IS your motivation.
In Jude, HE IS the foundation of your faith.
In Revelation, HE IS your coming King.

What is your favorite way to feel God's love in your own life?

* *Assignment Whisper* *

February 2

Tell your spouse that you love him or her in a new and unusual way today. Make sure that your other half knows that you do not take him or her for granted. Do not wait for Valentine's Day to send your sweetheart a store-bought card. Do something today that will touch your spouse's heart.

If you are not married or do not currently have a serious relationship that is leading toward marriage, prayerfully ask God to show love to your future spouse and/or your ex-spouse.

Some ideas to show love to your spouse are:

❖ Send a card to the office of your spouse.
❖ Cook him or her a favorite breakfast.
❖ Do that special morning ritual that you did when you were first married.
❖ Complete an errand or chore that your sweetheart does not enjoy.
❖ Fill your loved one's car with gas and get the oil changed.
❖ Buy a funny pen that will make your spouse smile.
❖ Is your husband a sports fan? Sit by his side and watch a game with him. Cook some hot dogs to eat on the sofa.
❖ Download a new song to an iPod that will remind him or her of you.
❖ Give your sweetheart a foot massage.
❖ Look him or her in the eye and express how loved your spouse makes you feel.
❖ Note your ideas here.

* *Assignment Whisper* *

February 3

Tell your children that you love them in a new and different way. Make sure they each know that you do not take them for granted. Tell your children how happy you are that they were born and how grateful you are that they are yours.

If you do not have children of your own, offer to babysit while a friend has a special outing with one of her children. It is not easy for parents to find time alone with each of their children. By entertaining one, you can provide that time for another child.

Consider spending time with your nieces and nephews making sure that they know how much you love them. If they live far away, try IM'ing them or creating a chat room. Send them a card or calling card so that they can call you.

Remember, the goal is for the child to feel loved and valued in your eyes. This does not necessarily require spending lots of money or hours of your time. It does, however, require sincerity.

February 4

You have just spent the past two days making sure that your spouse and children know that you do not take them for granted. This might have prompted thoughts about other people in your life who appear to take you for granted. Spend quality time praying for that person(s) today. Then do something nice for the person in your life that you take for granted the most. Show them love.

If you cringe at the thought, take heart. Most people who take you for granted expect you to do things for them. If you think about it for a minute, however, you might notice a pattern that you only respond to that person when they ask. Today, do something because you value that person. Trust me, they will not be expecting it, and because of that, you might get an unexpected reaction.

After today, do your best to resist taking advantage of people. One of my vows is never to ask another person to do something I am not willing to do myself. Notice I said "not willing to do." That is not the same thing as needing help or not having time to lend a hand. If you are about to ask someone to do something that would make you hold your breath, then refrain from asking. Consider the other person before opening your mouth or writing the email. Be aware of how your actions might take advantage of another person.

February 5

Who is the person in your life who would be thinking you were the ungrateful person in *their* life? Who is the person you call when you need assistance? Who is the person that you know will never tell you no? Hopefully, these questions produced a short list of names.

Today, go out of your way to thank the person(s). Make sure that they know how much they do for you and how much you love them for their devotion to you. Let them know that you realize their value in your life and how important they are. Say the words and mean it from your heart.

From today forward, remind yourself to think twice before asking these people for more help than they are able to give. Be sure that your future actions demonstrate that you remember today.

* *Assignment Whisper* *

February 6

Assignment Whisper was born following my birthday party in 2008. I decided to hold my birthday party at Build-A-Bear. My friends, ages 4 to 70, sang silly songs, danced goofy dances, and donated bears to the charity of my choosing. Together we donated 95 bears to the Texas Children's Hospital cancer unit. A few months later, another 15 bears were donated to the local Fisher House. It was the best birthday party I ever had!

Each year, my birthday party continues this theme of giving to others. The bears may continue or the gift may vary depending on the need. God will lead me each year to the need.

Since my birthday is close, now is the time to visit my website for details about the next event. Please check the website at www.assignmentwhisper.com for information on this year's festivities and recipients. Rest assured that the website will suggest ways for you to be involved, too!

* *Assignment Whisper* *

February 7

Tell your pharmacist that they are doing a great job.

Perhaps you are a frequent customer, or maybe you spend more time at the local vitamin store than the pharmacy. Even the healthiest person visits a pharmacist at some point in their life.

Stop by their counter today, or go through the drive-up window just to say thank you.

Here are some ideas to brighten their day:

- ❖ Take cookies.
- ❖ Write a thank you note. Deliver it in person or put it in the mail.
- ❖ Cut a bouquet of fresh flowers if you have a garden.
- ❖ Bring your children to sing a cheerful song.
- ❖ Donate a bottle of hand lotion; handling paper can cause dry skin.
- ❖ Order pizza delivered for lunch.
- ❖ Note your ideas here.

Assignment Whisper *

February 8

Volunteering Fact

According to www.worldvolunteerweb.org:
"Young people volunteered at twice the rate of adults with 55 percent of young people volunteering, compared with only 29 percent of adults."

Set a good example. Provide your children the opportunity to volunteer.

This may be more difficult with younger children. However, it is important to model this to children before they hit their teen years. Show them it is part of life.

If you want until their teen years to introduce the idea, they might feel as if you are trying to influence their behavior. Most parents realize just how much teens do not want their parents' influence. (Heaven forbid!)

* *Assignment Whisper* *

February 9

Write a thank you note to the author of your favorite book or your child's favorite book.

You will sometimes hear authors tell about the volume of letters they receive or how frequently their websites are visited. However, can you name anyone who has actually written to their favorite author? It seems to me that if that many people were writing, statistically speaking, by now we each would have met someone who really did it.

Today, be one of those people. Most everyone has a favorite author or a book that has inspired them. Write a brief thank you note to the author. Tell them how much you appreciate their work. Tell them how it changed your life.

If you write to the author of your child's book, ask your child to draw a picture of their favorite part of the book. If your child wrote a book report for school, include that assignment with the thank you note.

February 10

Compliment the cook at your favorite restaurant today.

Cooks are rarely seen. Their work holds them in the kitchen, away from the opportunity to see the people enjoying the fruits of their labor. Ask to speak to the chefs or write a note. Make them realize that they are not forgotten and are appreciated.

Valentine's Day and Mother's Day fill restaurants to capacity. The cooks would probably rather dine with their spouse, girlfriend/boyfriend, fiancé, or mother on these special occasions, too. Despite this fact, they work tirelessly so that we can have our special moments, creating memories with our loved ones.

Remember you favorite cook today.

February 11

Happy Birthday to you! Wait a minute. Did I get the date wrong?

For the most part, we know the birthdays of our closest friends. However, many special dates remain a mystery. How do you ask someone their date of birth when you should know already? You do not want to leave the impression that you were not paying attention.

Today, send birthday cards to those people. Be creative and silly to express your confusion. Have a good laugh over celebrating the birthday twice in one year. Once they receive the card, hopefully they will tell you the correct date.

I also encourage you to do this through the mail with a handwritten note instead of an email. Make it personal as well as comical.

February 12

Investigate the agency United Through Reading. Their website is www.unitedthroughreading.org.

If you have any children's books that your kids have outgrown, donate the books to this cause. If you do not have children, consider purchasing a book to donate. Discount bookstores and library sales provide affordable options for donations.

There are also several military bases who support this program as a way for deployed soldiers to stay in contact with their children.

For more information, visit this website: www.uso.org/whatwedo/specialprograms/unitedthr oughreading/.

February 13

Do something for a neighbor today who might be forgotten on Valentine's Day.

Do you know an elderly neighbor or one who lives alone? Take a card or some cookies. Make this person feel special and remembered.

Perhaps there is a mother on your block who has little support from her husband or family. Invite her over for coffee and a chat. In past generations, woman would chat over the clothesline while hanging laundry out to dry. You do not need a clothesline to be neighborly, however.

Maybe there is a neighbor whom you see walking his or her pet every day, but you never find the time to chat. Join this neighbor for a walk today. Remember that it does not matter what you discuss; the goal is to pay attention to that person. Let the spirit of Valentine's Day show in your attentiveness.

February 14

Valentine's Day. A day of love.

Everyone wants to be loved. The Bible employs several different words for love. The one that is most relevant to our lives, however, is agape love. The reason I stress the importance of agape love lies in the fact that is the most lasting and permanently impacting force in our lives. Other types of love come and go, but agape love sustains through time.

It is helpful to realize that agape love is a verb – not an emotion. Our society today portrays love as an emotion, something intense and momentary. Biblical love, agape love, involves action. It requires commitment, relationship, and purpose.

Webster defines "love" as "to hold dear, to cherish." Perhaps this is why it is often confused with an emotion. However, even Webster labels love as a verb.

Today while you are distributing Valentine's, prayerfully consider the Biblical definition of "love" and use love properly in your life.

February 15

Take adhesive bandages to your local florists.

After all the Valentine roses, their fingers might need them! If their fingers do not need them, the idea will put a smile on their face anyway.

When I was in grade school, I worked part time at the local floral shop. Every holiday created a frenzy of activity. The day after a holiday like Valentine's Day was just as busy.

The day following a holiday requires cleaning up, reorganizing, ordering new inventory, and restocking other supplies. All of this is accomplished while filling new orders and making sure the plants have enough water to survive! Any business that sells living things cannot rest for a moment and stay in business.

While you might be thinking that your florist is breathing a sigh of relief that Valentine's Day is past, their workload continues. Adhesive bandages bring relief to their fingers as well as a chuckle to their exhausted hands.

February 16

<u>Book recommendation</u>
Gary Chapman wrote these as well as other wonderful books on to topic of love.

The Five Love Languages: How to Express Heartfelt Commitment To Your Mate
The Five Love Languages, Men's Addition
The Five Love Languages of Children
The Five Love Languages of Teenagers
The Five Love Languages of Singles
The Heart of the Five Love Languages

Depending on your situation, one or all of these books might be appropriate. Encourage your spouse to read one with you. Discuss together what you learned about yourselves as well as each other.

If you have children, encourage your older children to read the adult version. Help them to determine what your love language is and how they can show it to you. You may need to remind them, however, that love is not a tool for manipulation. Communication remains the goal!

* *Assignment Whisper* *

February 17

"Why is it that God so often breaks our hearts?

"Well. Sometimes He does it to increase our faith. That's the way He stretches us. But there's another reason, I think, why our hearts get broken."

She looked at him.

"Usually," he said, "what breaks is what's brittle."

She nodded thoughtfully. "So we have to be careful of getting hard-hearted?"

"Bingo," he said, putting his arm around her shoulders as they walked to the end of the hall.

These High, Green Hills
by Jan Karon
page 301

Do you have situations or people in your life who make you feel hard-hearted or brittle? Do you struggle with the manner God uses to stretch your faith? Do you wish it were easier to not feel broken or lost?

Spend some time in prayer today asking God to show you those situations and people that He is using to reinforce your faith. Often times, the answer to our prayers are the hardest things to assimilate into our lives. Ask God for help. He will show you how to be strong and courageous at all times.

February 18

Thank the coaches of any child's sports team today.

If your kids enjoy watching sports more than playing, send a thank you note to your local YMCA. Most coaches take regular verbal abuse from parents. At the same time, most coaches are volunteers. How many volunteers do you know who enjoy being verbally abused?

Give them some happy words and a pretty smile. Take your children with you while you express your appreciation for all that they do.

Here are some ideas to brighten their day:

- ❖ Take cookies.
- ❖ Write a thank you note. Deliver it in person or put it in the mail.
- ❖ Cut a bouquet of fresh flowers if you have a garden.
- ❖ Bring your children to sing cheerful songs.
- ❖ Donate bottled water.
- ❖ Order pizza delivered for lunch.
- ❖ Note your ideas here.

February 19

Volunteer at a prison ministry.

There are many ways to do this, and not all of them involve actually entering a prison. If you feel called to perform volunteer hours in a prison or jail, contact the facility's chaplain to start the process.

Prison ministries do more than take the Gospel inside the walls. There are programs which assist children as they adjust to having an incarcerated parent. Fundraisers provide money to purchase supplies for inmates. People of all faiths assist with programs provided by ministries in a way that is compatible with their own beliefs.

If you are interested in ways to help prisoners from home, start with these websites for some ideas:

❖http://prisonministry.net/

❖www.pfm.org/default_pf_org.asp

Assignment Whisper

February 20

Most people enjoy chocolate during February. For some people, this indulgence risks their health. Eating disorders damage more lives today than just five short years ago.

Today, consider reaching out to those who struggle with eating disorders. For volunteer ideas, visit www.nationaleatingdisorders.org. According to this website:

"Our organization is dedicated to providing education, resources and support to those affected by eating disorders. Whether you are an individual living with an eating disorder, a family member or friend looking to offer support to a loved one, or a treatment professional looking to help others — we have structured our site to address your needs."

If your heart leans toward helping those with eating disorders, helping their families, or doing work behind the scenes, this organization has several options for you.

February 21

Be a baby holder at the local neonatal intensive care unit.

Often when babies are in the NICU, their parents are not able to spend much time with them. Their mothers may still be in the hospital themselves. Siblings need attention. People must return to work. There are countless reasons why families cannot spend large amounts of time in the hospital.

Baby holders fill that gap. Training is provided by the hospital, and no medical experience is required. This is also a good volunteer option for people who are only available during the evening hours as the NICU is just as active in the evening as in the daytime.

February 22

Thank a nurse at the local nursing home, hospice, or hospital.

February can be an unsettling time for residents of these facilities. Caregivers absorb the atmosphere and can become despondent when the residents are sad and lonely. Put a smile on their faces by letting them know that their efforts are not forgotten.

Here are some ideas to brighten their day:

- ❖ Take cookies.
- ❖ Write a thank you note. Deliver it in person or put it in the mail.
- ❖ Cut a bouquet of fresh flowers if you have a garden.
- ❖ Bring your children to sing cheerful songs.
- ❖ Donate a bottle of hand lotion as frequent washing dries the skin.
- ❖ Order pizza delivered for lunch.
- ❖ Note your ideas here.

February 23

Dress up as a clown and entertain kids at the local hospital.

Professional experience is not required. You do not even need a heart for clowning. Clowns generate laughs and giggles when making mistakes. Big red noses are easy to find at local party stores. Paint your face and leave your self-consciousness at home. The kids will love it!

Many party stores have simple magic tricks as well. Visit www.kidzone.ws/magic/ for tips on card tricks. If you play an instrument, sing with the kids. Audience participation shows are a big hit.

Remember that the goal remains to entertain sick children, not become an professional clown.

This idea also works well for a nursing home or hospice.

February 24

Volunteer to babysit for a mother who needs to go to the dentist or doctor today. The mother might be a friend, your sister, your sister-in-law, or a neighbor.

Reliable babysitters are hard to find during daytime hours. The best sitters are in school or involved with extracurricular activities when the dentist office is open. Offering this to your female friends provides them time to take care of themselves.

For the married men reading this book, offer to take time off work so that your wife can go to a dentist or doctor visit. Offer this before she has to ask. Make it clear that her health is important to you. It is a wonderful gift for a mother to be able to go to the dentist without worrying about the kids or whether she trusts the babysitter.

February 25

Thank a farmer today. If you do not know a farmer, contact a librarian or real estate agent of a small town.

Thank the farmer for growing your food.

Thank the famer for taking the risk each year that the weather will not wipe out the crop.

Thank a dairy farmer for all the vacations he missed because the cows have to be milked twice a day.

Thank the organic farmers for their commitment to growing healthy foods.

Thank a chicken farmer for each peck he got from an angry chicken.

Spend this day appreciating how your food arrived in your house and be thankful for the farmer who helped make it happen.

* *Assignment Whisper* *

February 26

Compliment a co-worker today.

There are people that we see every day at work. Most jobs have their own structure or repetition. It is easy to ignore opportunities to flatter people if it is not already built into the structure of your duties. Today, make the time to praise a co-worker. Surprise someone!

If you do not work outside the home, compliment someone who does something for you today. This might be the mail carrier, the grocery store clerk, or the gas station attendant. There are always people in our day who help us in some way.

Ask your children to join the fun. Offer a small reward for the child who gives the most smiles and good wishes. Make it a game and light up your world!

February 27

<u>Jesus Loves Me</u>
Author Unknown

Jesus loves me, this I know,
Though my hair is white as snow.
Though my sight is growing dim,
Still He bids me trust in Him.

(CHORUS)
Yes, Jesus loves me
Yes, Jesus loves me
Yes, Jesus loves me
For the Bible tells me so

Though my steps are oh, so slow,
With my hand in His I'll go.
On through life, let come what may,
He'll be there to lead the way.

(CHORUS)

Though I am no longer young,
I have much which He's begun.
Let me serve Christ with a smile,
Go with others the extra mile.

(CHORUS)

When the nights are dark and long,
In my heart He puts a song.
Telling me in words so clear,
"Have no fear, for I am near."

(CHORUS)

* *Assignment Whisper* *

When my work on earth is done,
And life's victories have been won.
He will take me home above,
Then I'll understand His love

(CHORUS)

I love Jesus, does He know?
Have I ever told Him so?
Jesus loves to hear me say,
That I love Him every day.

How did you tell Jesus that you love him today?

February 28

At work today, complete that task that everyone knows you avoid.

❖Make coffee.

❖Refill the paper tray in the copier.

❖Refill the water cooler.

❖Replace the toner cartridge.

❖Sweep the break room floor.

Take your turn at the dreaded task with a smile on your face. You might just discover that it is not so bad after all.

If you do not work outside the house, identify that task at home that your spouse does because you do not like to do it. Complete that task without being asked. Take the burden from your spouse for a day. Do *not* do it for recognition or manipulation.

* *Assignment Whisper* *

March 1

Spend some time studying and understanding God's purpose for your life.

This task might feel overwhelming. Bookstores sell countless books on the topic. You might choose to read some. However, the Bible obviously provides the best source.

In my humble opinion, the Bible teaches that our purpose is to glorify God. We are created to worship Him. In that regard, we are all created equal. However, the manner in which that purpose manifests itself exposes some differences.

Paul explains this best in I Corinthians 12. Verse 6 reminds us that, **"There are different kinds of working, but the same God works all of them in all men."** Then Paul goes on to explain the importance of each individual's gifts. Read the remainder of I Corinthians 12, and you will see that even though we each have our own unique contributions, our overall purpose remains the same – to glorify God.

I hope that by this point you feel more comfortable in whispering God's presence to others. Take a few moments today to fully appreciate your purpose.

March 2

Do something for or with your spouse that you do not want to do.

We all have those tasks that bring out the procrastinator in us. Yes, we remember that our spouse has asked us repeatedly to do that one little, pesky thing. For some reason probably unknown to even ourselves, we conveniently forget.

Today is the day. Just do it. There is no need to even discuss it with your spouse. Just surprise him or her by doing it. You will feel just as good about your accomplishment as you do about pleasing your other half.

* *Assignment Whisper* *

March 3

Do something for your kids that you have been putting off for no reason.

This might be something as simple as going to the park, or it may be more involved like buying that pet gerbil they have been begging for since last Christmas. Whatever it is, make that your primary purpose for the day. Surprise them.

If you have several children, it might be more practical to pick something that they all would enjoy. If they each have smaller items on their minds, try one each week until everyone has had a turn. The purpose here is to answer the call. Make them realize that you heard them and respond to them.

If you do not have children, borrow a niece or nephew today. Perhaps there is someone else who immediately comes to mind.

* *Assignment Whisper* *

March 4

Calling all skippers and captains! Lift the anchor, hoist the sails, and pray the boat remains afloat!

If that boat, truck, or recreational vehicle makes your spouse groan each time you pull into the driveway, call Boat Angels today. This organization refurbishes boats for resale. The proceeds finance projects such as funding medical operations and training, providing literature to prisons, and responding to world emergencies.

Boat Angels website outlines the procedure for donations. Visit www.boatangel.com for details. Pick up services are provided when necessary.

Although cash does not change hands for donations, charitable contribution forms are provided to comply the IRS regulations. Visit the link provided on the home page to learn how the IRS rules apply to your particular donation.

For those of you who are looking to purchase a boat, truck, or recreational vehicle, browse the inventory of this organization before chatting with local retailers. There might be a dream deal just waiting for you. Since the proceeds benefit a charity, everyone wins.

* *Assignment Whisper* *

March 5

Today remind yourself that this is *Assignment Whisper*. Redirect your purpose to whispering God's love, not shout it to the rooftops. If you are starting to feel proud of yourself, stop. On March 1, we looked at God's purpose for our lives. The glory goes to God, not ourselves. If you are feeling pompous and conceited for all that you have done for others this year, shift your focus. Take today to regroup.

Webster defines the word "whisper" as:
"to speak softly with little or no vibration of the vocal cords especially to avoid being overheard"

If your successes in whispering puff you up, you are vibrating too much!

In I Kings 19:12, the word "whisper" is translated as "thin, small, gaunt." Let God be the only thing "big" in your efforts.

If your whispering vibrations are under control, spend some time today taking note of how you keep them that way. You might need your own advice before the year is over.

March 6

Thank a police officer today.

Yes, police often arrive when you do not want one to notice you. Yet the men and women of our police force are forgotten heroes in most cities today. They routinely put their lives on the line for each of us and still their name alone can make people nervous.

Here are some ideas to brighten their day:

- ❖ Take cookies to the police station.
- ❖ Write a thank you note. Deliver it in person or put it in the mail.
- ❖ Cut a bouquet of fresh flowers for their lobby if you have a garden.
- ❖ Bring your children to sing cheerful songs.
- ❖ Order pizza delivered for lunch.
- ❖ Donate auto air fresheners.
- ❖ Donate your favorite CD's for their listening pleasure while on patrol.
- ❖ Note your ideas here.

* *Assignment Whisper* *

March 7

Leave a note or treat for the trash men today.

Imagine the world with no trash collection or dumps. Most urban areas have home pick up for trash. Regardless of the weather, trash collection occurs on a reliable and predictable schedule.

Some rural areas require home owners to make trips to the dump themselves. These home owners spend more time in their disposal of household trash. When they arrive at the dump, employees still assist them.

Write a thank you note to your trash collectors or dump employees today. Put it in a boldly marked envelope and tape it to your trash can. You could also attach the envelop to a box of cookies or water bottles. Whatever you do, they will appreciate being remembered and noticed. If possible, watch their reaction from your window.

March 8

Thank your pastor today.

If you really think about it, a pastor's job is almost as thankless as that of a police officer. If we truly understood everything that a pastor does for their congregation, most of us would develop a headache and feel fatigued half way through the list. You do not have to understand it all to acknowledge the person. Take time today to tell your pastor how much you respect him/her for their dedication, commitment, and sacrifices.

Here are some ideas to brighten their day:

- ❖ Take cookies.
- ❖ Write a thank you note. Deliver it in person or put it in the mail.
- ❖ Cut a bouquet of fresh flowers if you have a garden.
- ❖ Bring your children to sing cheerful songs.
- ❖ Donate a box of facial tissues. Think of how many people cry in the pastor's office!
- ❖ Order pizza delivered for lunch.
- ❖ Note your ideas here.

March 9

Encourage a teen today.

If you have a child who is a teen, today is the day to encourage that person. Too often in our society, we get hurried and inconsiderate by default. Take the time today to listen to the tone of what comes out of your mouth when you are around your teen. Make sure that all of your words are encouraging thoughts and uplifting sentiments. Yes, do this even with the most frustrating of teens! Let your positive feelings turn their attitudes around before they notice what hit them!

Consider your child's opinion of your general mood when you talk. Most parents believe that teens pay no attention to their parents. However, when they are adults, they will remember an overall attitude of their home life. Pay attention today to what atmosphere you project in your home by what you say. Will your teen aged children remember their home as a place of encouragement or criticism? Will they remember opening the door to laughter or tension?

If you do not have children of your own, call a niece or nephew. You can also chose a neighbor or friend's teenager.

Create a joyful childhood for your children on purpose. Commit your mouth as well as your heart to a future full of happy memories.

March 10

Volunteer at Meals on Wheels today.

This organization does not always require large amounts of time from their volunteers. If you only have a few hours to spare, ask what you can contribute with in a minimal amount of time.

Visit www.mowaa.org today to discover more information. This website states:

"The Meals On Wheels Association of America (MOWAA) is the oldest and largest organization in the United States representing those who provide meal services to people in need. Our mission is to provide visionary leadership and professional training and to develop partnerships that will ensure the provision of quality nutrition services to seniors in need."

* *Assignment Whisper* *

March 11

Donate blood today.

Donating blood takes approximately thirty minutes. Within 24 hours of your donation, your blood impacts the lives of three people. If you are a rare blood type, you will probably save someone's life by your donation.

In most locations, donation with parental consent starts at age 16. Although small children are not allowed in the draw area, it is common for blood centers to have play areas for your children to use while you donate. To top it off, they have snacks!

If you are apprehensive about donating, I strongly encourage you to try it anyway. The staff have experience dealing with nervous people. Honestly, it is not as bad as you might imagine. The whole process concludes before you have time to sweat.

If medical issues prevent you from donating blood, consider other ways to volunteer. Organize a blood drive at your church or school. Donate toys to their play area. Stuff flyers into envelops. Be a graphic artist for other drives.

Contact your local Red Cross or hospital to find a donation center as well as other volunteer ideas.

* *Assignment Whisper* *

March 12

Check your perspective today. Whenever you are disappointed with your spot in life, think about little Jamie.

Jamie was trying out for a part in the school play. His mother said that he had set his heart on being in it, though she feared he would not be chosen. On the day the parts were awarded, she went to collect him after school. Jamie rushed up to her, eyes shining with pride and excitement.

"Guess what, Mom," he shouted, and then said those words that will remain a lesson to me....."I've been chosen to clap and cheer."

What things make you frown? What things lift your spirits?

If your purpose in life excludes menial tasks, reevaluate your definition of purpose. Everyone learns valuable lessons from their time in the clap and cheer section.

March 13

Do something for another neighbor today.

You will notice that I encourage you to meet your immediate neighbors throughout this devotional. It is important to know our community. Just one generation ago, neighbors knew all of their neighbors. Even if they were not friends, everyone knew who lived in every house or apartment and more importantly, who did not belong there. When I was a child, every mother on the block had at least one opportunity to bandage my skinned knees. We never thought of going all the way home when we knew every mother on the block.

Imagine the world that way again. Do something today that will set that in motion. Make it a goal to meet all of your neighbors before the National Night Out in the fall. Create safe neighborhoods on purpose.

March 14

Volunteer at your child's school today.

Most public and private schools can use an extra pair of hands. Some schools create organized systems for volunteers to be involved in their kids' activities. Ask how you can help for a day or on a regular basis.

If you homeschool, assign one of your children to be the teacher for the day so that you can volunteer to help them. The change of pace might be a fun adventure for all of you.

If you do not have children, see if it is possible to volunteer at the school of a niece, nephew, or neighbor. Some schools have strict policies about who is allowed in contact with the students. There may be other things, however, that you can do for the school. Ask to speak to the volunteer coordinator to brainstorm ideas.

* *Assignment Whisper* *

March 15

Do something nice for a janitor today. You can find janitors almost anywhere: your office building, a school, the mall, the local movie theater, the grocery store, etc.

Here are some ideas to brighten their day:

❖ Write a thank you note. Deliver it in person or tape it to the cleaning board found in most public restrooms.

❖ Take them a box of cookies.

❖ Cut a bouquet of fresh flowers if you have a garden.

❖ Bring your children to sing cheerful songs.

❖ Donate a bottle of hand lotion; cleaning solutions damage skin.

❖ Buy them lunch, or give them a gift certificate for a local restaurant.

❖ Note your ideas here.

* *Assignment Whisper* *

March 16

Remember a farmer's wife today.

They make many sacrifices and work hard on their farms just as their husband's do. Their lives revolve around planting seasons and milking schedules. Their prosperity depends on the weather and Mother Nature. They can be unexpectedly robbed of quality time with their husband because of a sick animal or broken machinery.

If you know a farmer's wife, it will be easy to come up with a fun idea to surprise her. Pick today to acknowledge her.

If you do not know a farmer's wife, pray for these women in general. Take some time to consider their lifestyle and how it impacts your world. Reflect on the sacrifices they make as well as their contributions to our world's food chain. Imagine what a grocery store would look like if there were no farmers and the wives who support them.

* *Assignment Whisper* *

March 17

Do something for a sibling today.

For some of you, this will be easy, fun, and exciting. Some of you know just what to do to make your siblings smile. Surprise them today and make them feel special.

If you do not have a good relationship with your siblings, begin a new tradition today. Try something that does not require their participation or reaction. Surprise them in a way that makes them know that you are thinking about them and care about them even if they do not want to acknowledge that fact.

If you have siblings who have died, spend some time in their favorite place or doing their favorite activity. You could also write a letter to them, recalling how much you enjoyed being their sibling. Keep their memory alive and pass it on to the next generation.

If you are an only child, apply these ideas to a cousin or close relative.

* *Assignment Whisper* *

March 18

Volunteering fact
According to www.worldvolunteerweb.org:
"Youth who volunteer are less likely to engage in risky behavior, are more likely to feel connected to their communities, and tend to do better in school."

Model your volunteering spirit to any teens that you know. Encourage them to feel connected to you and their community. Help them to understand that you want their lives to be happy and prosperous. Present alternatives to wasting their lives on drugs, criminal activities, or unrealistic goals.

Showing kids that they are a part of their community teaches them to value other people. It also creates opportunities for other people to demonstrate that they value the teens.

Let the teens see how their performance in school affects the community, both positively and negatively. Assist them in finding purpose in their lives. Walk with them on their path to success.

* *Assignment Whisper* *

March 19

Do something for mentally challenged people today.

Mentally challenged people often feel isolated, especially in smaller communities. People are confused about how to talk to them. Even people who appear to be low functioning still have feelings and hobbies. They still enjoy attention.

Try to spend some time with mentally challenged people today and see them as Jesus sees them. They were given their unique personalities for a reason. Ask God to show you His gifts to these people.

> **As he [Jesus] went along, he saw a man blind from birth.**
>
> **His disciples asked him, "Rabbi, who sinned, this man or his parents, that he was born blind?"**
>
> **"Neither this man nor his parents sinned," said Jesus, "but this happened so that the work of God might be displayed in his life. As long as it is day, we must do the work of him who sent me. Night is coming, when no one can work. While I am in the world, I am the light of the world."**
>
> **John 9:1-5**

Did you catch that? "...so that the work of God might be displayed in his life..."

You may know someone personally who could use some cheer today, or you may need to contact your local community center for ideas. If this task feels outside of your comfort zone, contact the local community center to see if there are ways to volunteer behind the scenes.

Be watchful of how God's work is displayed.

* *Assignment Whisper* *

March 20

Since there is no way to know what year you are reading this devotional, the exact date of Easter remains a mystery. Therefore, this recipe for Resurrection Rolls is included now in the hope that Easter's arrival is emanate.

<u>Resurrection Rolls</u>
Author Unknown

Here's a new twist on the Resurrection Cookie idea for Easter, both are recipes you can do with your kids or grand kids in order for them to understand the death and resurrection of Jesus Christ. This fun recipe uses Crescent rolls and a disappearing marshmallow!

Preheat Oven to 350 degrees
Ingredients:
Crescent rolls
Melted butter
Large marshmallows
Cinnamon
Sugar

Give each child a triangle of crescent rolls. The crescent roll represents the cloth that Jesus was wrapped in.

Read Matthew 27:57-61

1. Give each child a marshmallow. This represents Jesus.
2. Have him/her dip the marshmallow in melted butter. This represents the oils of embalming.

3. Now dip the buttered marshmallow in the cinnamon and sugar which represents the spices used to anoint the body.

4. Then wrap up the coated marshmallow tightly in the crescent roll (not like a typical crescent roll up, but bring the sides up and seal the marshmallow inside.) This represents the wrapping of Jesus' body after death.

5. Place in a 350 degree oven for 10-12 minutes. (The oven represents the tomb - pretend like it was three days!)

6. Let the rolls cool slightly. The children can open their rolls (cloth) and discover that Jesus is no longer there, HE IS RISEN!!!! (The marshmallow melts and the crescent roll is puffed up, but empty.)

Now read Matthew 28:5-8.

Explain: At the tomb, Mary Magdalene and the other Mary saw an angel, who told them not to be afraid. No one had taken Jesus' body, but He Had risen from the dead! The angel told the women to go and tell the disciples what they had seen, that Jesus had risen from the dead. They were so excited, they ran all the way home to tell the disciples the good news! He is risen from the dead! Alleluia!

After that Jesus appeared in person to Peter, then to the 12 disciples and after that, to more than 500 people. Jesus' appearance to eyewitnesses, those who saw Him with their own eyes, would give support and prove that Jesus rose from the dead (1 Corinthians 15:3-6).

By rising from the dead, Jesus proved once and for all that He was the Messiah, the Savior of the World, the Chosen One, and the Lamb of God. By dying on the cross and rising from the dead, Jesus did what no other had ever done before. As both God and man, He overcame sin, death, and hell.

* *Assignment Whisper* *

And now because of what Jesus has done, these things no longer have any power over those who believe in Jesus and allow His Spirit to lead and direct them. Rather than being slaves to sin and death, Christians (those who love and believe in Jesus) are free to obey God and do good (Romans 6:17-18). The Bible says in John 8:36, "If therefore the Son shall make you free, you shall be free indeed."

However, we will only obey God if we listen to the Holy Spirit our helper. He enables believers in Jesus to do the right thing. It is important that we read the Bible (God's Word) because one of the ways the Holy Spirit helps us obey God is by reminding us of what He says to us in His Word. God's Spirit will never go against his Word. In fact, when we read God's Word, we are listening to the Holy Spirit. Of course, you won't always do the right thing; the Bible says this (1 John 1:5-10). But that is why we need to continue to confess our sins knowing that God forgives us, based on what Jesus did on the cross. This is also a reason we need to spend time with other believers in Christ so they can encourage us in our faith.

May you have a blessed and meaningful Easter!

March 21

Compliment your mother's cooking today.

Most mothers spend a considerable amount of their lives in the kitchen. They cook. They clean. They pretend to wash the counters as they eaves drop on their children with their friends. For some mothers, cooking is a pleasure; for others, it is a chore. Either way, cooking meals for the family occupies many hours of her day.

Ask your mother for one of her recipes today. Tell her the fond memories you have of her in the kitchen. Remind her of a time that she cooked a special meal for you. It will mean the world to her that you remembered her thoughtfulness.

If your mother was not a good cook, then remind her of a special time at a restaurant or special celebration that you cherish.

If your mother is not alive, write her a letter. Relive the happy memory and preserve it to share with the next generation. If you know some of her recipes, document them for your children. Integrate sharing the past with your children part of your purpose in life.

* *Assignment Whisper* *

March 22

Thank your parents today for raising you.

Remember that your parents made a choice. The options of adoption or abortion existed in past generations. We often like to think that our ancestors were better at planning their children to achieve the American dream. Most of us have heard the "two kids, a station wagon, and a dog inside the picket fence" version of the American Dream from our parents or grandparents.

Other mothers in past generations had enormous struggles in their pregnancies. Medical science was not as well equipped fifty years ago to deal with complications during pregnancy. Those who desired children did not always have an easy time achieving that dream. Yet here we are.

Even if you feel that your parents did a poor job of parenting, they still rose to the occasion. You are still here because of what they did and the sacrifices they made.

Today, tell both of your parents how much you appreciate their decision to raise you.

March 23

Gamers unite! Today is playing day.

Visit www.childsplaycharity.org for a very unique way to help children.

Their website describes their goal:
"Child's Play Charity was established in 2003. It is a community based charity that provides toys, games, books and cash donations to children's' hospitals across the world."

Let all of those hours playing video games inspire you to participate in this organization's activities. What fun to share your love of gaming with others! If you thought volunteering was hard work, today is your chance to play and still do something nice for someone else.

If gaming is not your passion, this site has other ideas to get involved and support their cause.

Include playing in your life's purpose today.

March 24

Write a thank you note to the author of your favorite cookbook.

Unless your name is Betty Crocker, chances are high that you have used a cookbook at some point in your life. Some people use them daily. For me, "cook" and "book" are four letter words to be avoided at all cost!

People seldom consider the work involved in publishing a cookbook. Chefs spend hours in their kitchens developing and refining new recipes to share. Next comes the organization and publication of the book itself. The entire process takes longer than some marriages last.

Take a moment now to locate the author's address or website. Send them a thank you note and mention the thing you like best about their cookbook. Mention which recipe is your favorite, too. Let them know that you appreciate the effort they put into creating their cookbook.

Assignment Whisper

March 25

Take an American Sign Language class.

Learning a second language is a necessity in this generation. Most universities require a foreign language for graduation. The majority of major metropolises in the world contain ethnic areas where English is rarely heard. In some regions of the United States, Spanish dominates over the English language. Yet few people consider ASL as a second language.

According to the National Institute of Deafness and Other Communication Disorders, approximately 17 percent (36 million) of American adults report some degree of hearing loss. About 2 to 3 out of every 1,000 children in the United States are born deaf or hard-of-hearing. Nine out of every 10 children who are born deaf are born to parents who can hear.

Take the time to learn some basic words and phrases of ASL today. Many community centers have classes. *The Joy of Signing* by Lottie Riekehof is also a helpful book to learn the basics.

March 26

Donate to Project Linus.

Visit their website for ways to donate www.projectlinus.org/.

This group appeals to quilters, knitters, and those handy with a crochet hook. Quilts created from any sort of craft are accepted.

Project Linus does not require finished projects. If you only have time to make a few squares, their volunteers join them to others and complete the quilts. If you make quilt tops, they stitch them to the back for you.

If craftiness eludes you, consider learning. Your local hobby store or fabric shops sell instructional books. Basic supplies are not expensive. Unlock your creativity!

* *Assignment Whisper* *

March 27

Thank your local librarian today.

It might appear that they spend their days in the calmness of a library, but librarian duties and the library's place in our society have changed over the years. Libraries of the last generation were a quiet place to study and read. Today they are more like internet cafes or community centers. The last time I visited the library, a group of musicians performed in the children's area while several patrons chattered on cell phones. Times have changed.

Through these changes, librarians adapt. They continue to answer questions and assist patrons no matter what transpires around them. They schedule community events, babysit neighborhood children, mediate computer usage time, and still memorize the Dewey Decimal System as well as the Library of Congress system. In my experience, they still possess the patience of the librarians of my youth.

Remind your librarians how much you appreciate their knowledge, fortitude, and willingness to adapt to the needs of the community. Remember to turn off your cell phone when you enter!

March 28

Do not let any unwholesome talk come out of your mouths, but only what is helpful for building others up according to their needs, that it may benefit those who listen.

Ephesians 4:29

What came out of your mouth today? Listen to yourself over the course of the day. Do your words uplift people, or do you need to check your tongue more often than you thought?

Do others the favor of choosing your words carefully. Ensure that your words and their tone project your purpose accurately.

March 29

Thank the UPS man today.

The UPS truck drivers are another one of those silent workers in our world. We do not really acknowledge them or value them. Yet consider the world without them. Think about how many times in their careers they have heard gratitude from their clients.

Let today be the day that they hear your gratitude. Here are some ideas to brighten their day:

❖ Offer a bottled drink for the road.

❖ Write a card.

❖ Bake cookies.

❖ Give adhesive bandages for blisters.

❖ Give colorful shoelaces (Imagine breaking a shoe lace in a job that involves so much walking.)

❖ Write encouraging words on a magnet for them to put on their dashboard.

You could also go to the UPS store nearest your home to say thank you. Visit www.ups.com for store locations.

* *Assignment Whisper* *

March 30

Things in motion tend to stay in motion.

Resolve to stay in motion with your whispering. Do not let the little things in life burden you. Let your whispering to others infuse energy into your soul. If you jotted down notes since starting this devotional, review your observations and remind yourself how wonderful it feels to whisper God's love to others.

When children get bored, they start to get naughty. Adults are the same way. Idleness leads to destructive paths regardless of your age. Make a commitment today to avoid that situation.

We do not want you to become lazy, but to imitate those who through faith and patience inherit what has been promised.

Hebrews 6:12

Lazy hands make a man poor, but diligent hands bring wealth.

Proverbs 10:4

* *Assignment Whisper* *

March 31

<u>Recipe for Peace</u>
Author Unknown

1 cup of friendship
1/2 cup of hope
2 cups of love
5 tbsp of respect
1/2 cup of kindness
1 cup of joy
3 tsp of understanding
1 1/2 cups honesty

1. Mix friendship, love, and kindness in large bowl.
2. Add understanding a few drops at a time.
3. Stir in honesty and joy for good firm dough.
4. Sprinkle half of respect over it and mix well.
5. Pour into a cake pan and bake at 350°F.
6. When it is ready, pour the hope and the rest of respect on top and share with everyone you know.

Serve peace to those in your path today. Make peace with your purpose in life and rededicate yourself to this idea.

* *Assignment Whisper* *

April 1

God's promises to us are too numerous to list here. Suffice to say that the Bible is full of promises and verification of God's commitment to you. Many times we read these promises as antidotes, sayings you might see on a cute plaque on a wall. Make no mistake. God takes His promises seriously. Do you?

Here are a couple of God's promises as they relate to giving. Let them inspire you to find other verses.

He who gives to the poor will lack nothing, but he who closes his eyes to them receives many curses.
Proverbs 28:27

Each man should give what he has decided in his heart to give, not reluctantly or under compulsion, for God loves a cheerful giver.
2 Corinthians 9:7

* *Assignment Whisper* *

April 2

Write a love letter reaffirming your commitment to your spouse today.

Include in your note some of the things that you promise to do or change. List the promises that your spouse has kept in your marriage and what these promises mean to you. Let your spouse know how much it means to you that you can depend on him or her and the commitment to your marriage.

If you are not married, write a letter to your future spouse. Document how you plan to fulfill your covenant to him or her. List the promises that you expect your spouse to make.

If your spouse assigns no value to commitment, do not despair! Read February 14 in this devotional again. Let the definition of agape love jog your memory regarding the things that your spouse contributes to honor the commitment he or she made on your wedding day.

April 3

Write a love letter to each of your kids today.

Tell them how committed you are to raising them to be wonderful people. Reaffirm your desire to be the best parent possible. Be specific. Writing the details provides clarity in your own mind as well as in the minds of your children.

Read these letters to your children as a family. Allowing everyone in the family to hear your letters holds you accountable for their content. This will encourage your children to do the same for you. You may need patience as you want for the impact on your family.

If you do not have children yet, write the letter to your future children. Give serious thought to the kind of parent that you want to be. Describe how you see yourself raising your children.

April 4

Learn the words to a new, cheerful song today.

Sing it in public with a smile on your face. This is easier to do if you have children, but go for it even without reinforcements.

You do not have to assemble an audience. Just sing and smile as you go about your day. Attitudes are infectious. Spread some antibiotic today through cheery song.

Some simples songs to try include:
  ❖ Jesus Loves Me
  ❖ Puff the Magic Dragon
  ❖ Theme song from your favorite television show
  ❖ Favorite Christmas song
  ❖ Hokie Pokie
  ❖ Happy Birthday

Singing cheerful songs will reinforce your commitment to whispering. Happiness spreads like wildfire. Commit yourself to being content not only for yourself, but for your family and friends as well. Whisper jubilation through your songs today.

April 5

And God said, "This is the sign of the covenant I am making between me and you and every living creature with you, a covenant for all generations to come: And God said, "This is the sign of the covenant I am making between me and you and every living creature with you, a covenant for all generations to come.. Whenever the rainbow appears in the clouds, I will see it and remember the everlasting covenant between God and all living creatures of every kind on the earth."

Genesis 9:12-13, 16

Did you know that the rainbow represents God's commitment to us? Watch for rainbows today, both real and figurative rainbows, and remember that God is faithful to His promises.

Let your actions today demonstrate commitment to your promises, too.

April 6

Learn the importance of covenant today.

The Bible frequently talks about covenant relationships. Marriage falls into the category of a covenant relationship. However, the Bible also talks of friendships this way.

The definition of "covenant" from the Hebrew:

1) covenant, alliance, pledge
   a) between men
      1) treaty, alliance, league (man to man)
      2) constitution, ordinance
         (monarch to subjects)
      3) agreement, pledge (man to man)
      4) alliance (of friendship)
      5) alliance (of marriage)
   b) between God and man
      1) alliance (of friendship)
      2) covenant (divine ordinance with signs or
         pledges)

Does your behavior demonstrate a covenant relationship with your spouse? With your children? With your closest friends? What needs to happen to change that?

April 7

Pray for the IRS staff and the lawmakers who write tax laws for our nation.

April is a difficult time for people in those jobs. They are human beings, too, and deserve respect and patience. The IRS staff did not write the laws. They are governed by these rules just as much as the rest of us. They do not have the option of enforcing only the laws that they like or that make sense or benefit you. They are just doing their job.

Put aside your feelings about the laws and taxes and see these folks as individuals. Pray for them during this stressful time of the year. They take more verbal abuse than most.

April 8

Thank your accountant today.

They are probably deprived of sleep. It is not their fault that tax time comes every year. Be kind to your tax preparation person and their staff today.

Here are some ideas to brighten their day:

- ❖ Take coffee to their office.
- ❖ Write a thank you note. Deliver it in person or put it in the mail.
- ❖ Cut a bouquet of fresh flowers if you have a garden.
- ❖ Bring your children to sing cheerful songs.
- ❖ Donate a bottle of hand lotion; handling papers can dry the skin.
- ❖ Donate pencils or a sharpener.
- ❖ Order pizza delivered for lunch.
- ❖ Note your ideas here.

April 9

Check your perception today.

Consider what the word "rich" means to you. Is "rich" only about money? Does "rich" make you smile or dream? Does the concept give you heart burn?

Most people who claim financial stability will tell you that there remains some area in their life that makes them feel poor. Perhaps they lack friends. Maybe a childhood dream eludes them despite their financial success. It is rare to meet someone who would claim to be "rich" in every aspect of their life.

Spend some time today detailing your definition of "rich" for your own life. What aspects of your life makes you "rich?" What goals still need reaching to complete the picture? What are you doing today to make those goals obtainable? Recommit to those goals and the work needed to get there.

April 10

Neighbor day arrives again.

Today choose a neighbor who is known to do things for everyone else in the vicinity. Most every neighborhood boasts one person that is always willing to contribute to any project. Thank that person today.

Here are some ideas to brighten their day:

- ❖ Invite them over for coffee.
- ❖ Babysit their kids one evening.
- ❖ Write a thank you note. Deliver it in person or put it in the mail.
- ❖ Give them fresh flowers from your garden.
- ❖ Sing a cheerful song with your children.
- ❖ Note your ideas here.

April 11

A tax assessor came one day to a poor Christian to determine the amount of taxes he would have to pay. The following conversation took place:

"What property do you possess?" asked the assessor.

"I am a very wealthy man," replied the Christian.

"List your possessions, please," the assessor instructed.

The Christian said:

> First, I have everlasting life, John 3:16
>
> Second, I have a mansion in heaven, John 14:2
>
> Third, I have peace that passes all understanding, Philippians 4:7
>
> Fourth, I have joy unspeakable, 1 Peter 1:8
>
> Fifth, I have divine love which never fails, 1 Corinthians 13:8
>
> Sixth, I have a faithful wife, Proverbs 31:10
>
> Seventh, I have healthy, happy obedient children, Exodus 20:12
>
> Eighth, I have true, loyal friends, Proverbs 18:24
>
> Ninth, I have songs in the night, Psalms 42:8
>
> Tenth, I have a crown of life, James 1:12"

The tax assessor closed his book, and said, "Truly you are a very rich man, but your property is not subject to taxation."

I pray that all of us will have this kind of tax free "wealth." Thanks for dropping in; Have a richly blessed day!

Consider if your heart is committed to things of this world or gifts from God. Does your heart focus on money and material possessions or ways to honor God?

April 12

Tax time produces stress. How many people do you know who enjoy talking about taxes and April 15th?

Consider the alternative. Think about the homeless people in your community. They are not worried about April 15th. Would you rather change places with them so that you do not have to think about taxes? They are not worried because they have nothing; others worry because they have too much.

Today let go of things of this world. Release yourself from the stress of tax time. Let go of the feeling of ownership of your material possessions. Recognize that all material possessions are temporary. They will all pass away.

I am not suggesting that you give all of your belongings to the poor. This is about emotionally releasing yourself from your property. Do not let the stress of tax time control your thoughts. Money is gift from God and does not belong to us. Remember - even Jesus paid taxes.

* *Assignment Whisper* *

April 13

But seek first the kingdom of God and His righteousness, and all these things shall be added to you.

Matthew 6:33

After releasing your emotional hold on your possessions yesterday, seeking the kingdom of God is the next step. Remember, God prepared a glorious place for us. There is no reason to hold on to the things of this earth so tightly.

Here is a joke to keep things in perspective:

One day a very wealthy man died. During his lifetime, he accumulated a large amount of money as well as every material possession that a person could have. Needless to say, he dreaded parting with his collection of wealth.

When the man arrived at the Pearly Gates, he begged St. Peter to allow him to bring everything with him into heaven. St. Peter refused his request and explained that those things were useless in heaven.

But the man persisted until St. Peter finally agreed to one suitcase. The man was thrilled. He returned to earth and filled his suitcase with bricks of gold. He could finally take his wealth with him!

When he arrived back at the Pearl Gates, St. Peter asked to see the contents of the suitcase. The man excitedly opened his valise.

When St. Peter saw the rows of gold bricks, he felt confused. He turned to the man and asked, "You could bring anything you wanted into heaven. Why did you bring ordinary street pavement?"

* *Assignment Whisper* *

April 14

Thank your gas station attendant today.

The days of full service gas stations on every corner disappeared, but gas stations still employ staff. Gas stations are not as safe as they were ten years ago either. Employees realize that their jobs involve more danger than other vocations. Not only do they deal with verbal abuse and complaints about the high price of gasoline, they also have to be watchful for burglars and violence between customers. Their job training includes more than making change.

Take a moment today to pay inside and thank the attendant. Say something cheerful or present a card or flowers. Whatever you decide will convey more recognition than this employee has probably received from a customer all year.

April 15

This is also why you pay taxes, for the authorities are God's servants, who give their full time to governing. Give everyone what you owe him: If you owe taxes, pay taxes; if revenue, then revenue; if respect, then respect; if honor, then honor.

Romans 13:6-7

No one can serve two masters. Either he will hate the one and love the other, or he will be devoted to the one and despise the other. You cannot serve both God and Money.

Matthew 6:24

For the love of money is a root of all kinds of evil. Some people, eager for money, have wandered from the faith and pierced themselves with many griefs.

I Timothy 6:10

Keep your lives free from the love of money and be content with what you have, because God has said, "Never will I leave you; never will I forsake you."

Hebrews 13:5

April 16

Pecans in the Cemetery
Author Unknown

On the outskirts of a small town, there was a big, old pecan tree just inside the cemetery fence.

One day, two boys filled up a bucketful of nuts and sat down by the tree, out of sight, and began dividing the nuts.

"One for you, one for me. One for you, one for me," said one boy. Several dropped and rolled down toward the fence.

Another boy came riding along the road on his bicycle. As he passed, he thought he heard voices from inside the cemetery. He slowed down to investigate.

Sure enough, he heard, "One for you, one for me. One for you, one for me." He just knew what it was. He jumped back on his bike and rode off.

Just around the bend he met an old man with a cane, hobbling along.

"Come here quick," said the boy, "you won't believe what I heard! Satan and the Lord are down at the cemetery dividing up the souls."

The man said, "Beat it kid, can't you see it's hard for me to walk." When the boy insisted though, the man hobbled slowly to the cemetery.

Standing by the fence they heard, "One for you, one for me. One for you, one for me..."

The old man whispered, "Boy, you've been tellin' me the truth. Let's see if we can see the Lord."

Shaking with fear, they peered through the fence, yet were still unable to see anything. The old man and the boy gripped the wrought iron bars of the fence tighter and tighter as they tried to get a glimpse of the Lord.

* *Assignment Whisper* *

At last they heard, "One for you, one for me. That's all. Now let's go get those nuts by the fence, and we'll be done."

They say the old man made it back to town a full five minutes ahead of the kid on the bike.

What are you believing today? Pay attention to the things you hear and what you believe. Are you remembering half truths? Are you misinterpreting the things people say to you? Do you miss the meaning behind the words?

Check your beliefs today. Realign them with God's truths.

* *Assignment Whisper* *

April 17

Make heart pillows today.

If you or someone you know survived breast cancer, you may be familiar with heart pillows. Their design makes a shape specifically to fit under the arm and promotes healing following surgery.

If you enjoy sewing, make a few pillows. If sewing machines intimidate you, donate fabric or stuffing. Volunteering to distribute them to patients requires no sewing skills.

This is not a ministry just for women. Men also contract breast cancer.

The heart pillows benefit others besides breast cancer survivors. Some pillows assist heart surgery patients. If you have a local hospital that specializes in cardiac surgeries, check with them for donation possibilities.

Visit www.heartpillow.dk for more information.

* *Assignment Whisper* *

April 18

Be a tutor.

Countless tutoring options exists across the globe, and not all of them involve books. You could volunteer to tutor a teen in their school work. Adult literacy programs need volunteers. Some areas of the country use tutors for classes in English as a Second Language for all ages.

If you are blessed with a musical talent, tutor kids on their instrument of choice or be an audience while they sing. Some kids just need encouragement or someone to count the beat for them.

If sports are your passion, volunteer to assist a coach in practices. Be that extra pair of hands on the field to encourage and support the kids.

Contact your local library, school, or community center for more information.

April 19

Clay Balls
Author Unknown

A man who was exploring caves by the seashore. In one of the caves he found a canvas bag with a bunch of hardened clay balls. It was like someone had rolled up clay and left them out in the sun to bake. They didn't look like much, but they intrigued the man so he took the bag out of the cave with him.

As he strolled along the beach, to pass the time, he would throw the clay balls one at a time out into the ocean as far as he could throw.

He thought little about it until he dropped one of the balls and it cracked open on a rock. Inside was a beautiful, precious stone.

Excited the man started breaking open the remaining clay balls. Each contained a similar treasure. He found thousands of dollars worth of jewels in the 20 or so clay balls he had left, then it struck him.

He had been on the beach a long time. He had thrown maybe 50 or 60 of the clay balls with their hidden treasure into the ocean waves. Instead of thousands of dollars in treasure, he could have taken home tens of thousands, but he just threw it away.

It's like that with people we look at someone, maybe even ourselves, and we see the external clay vessel. It doesn't look like much from the outside. It isn't always beautiful or sparkling, so we discount it, we see that person as less important than someone more beautiful or stylish or well known or wealthy. But we have not taken the time to find the treasure hidden inside that person by God.

There is a treasure in each and every one of us. If we take the time to get to know that person, and if we ask God to show us that person the way He sees them, then the clay begins to peel away and the brilliant gem begins to shine forth. May we not come to the end of our lives and find out that we have thrown away a fortune in friendships because the gems were hidden in bits of clay. May we see the people in our world as God sees them. Life is great when you have friends.

What or who did you discard today?

April 20

Vroom!!! Vroom!!!

Motorcycles are not just for transportation any more. You would be amazed at the number of motorcycle clubs that engage in regular volunteer work. If you are a rider or enthusiast, this idea is perfect for you.

Visit this website for information:

www.tiac.net/~mpbcds/motorcycle_ministries.htm.

This site lists groups all over the globe that do a wide variety of ministry projects. Whether you are looking for ways to ride while delivering donations or want to do prison ministry with your group, this site provides valuable information to start your engines.

Put on your helmet and grab your sunglasses. Today's volunteer idea rolls outdoors!

* *Assignment Whisper* *

April 21

Pet lovers unite!

Volunteer to babysit a pet for a friend or neighbor who is going on vacation this summer. Volunteer before they ask.

Some pets are easy. Goldfish take virtually no effort, but it is no fun for kids to come home to a dead goldfish. There are kennels for dogs and cats, but not all pets have a day care option. Tell your friend now that they can depend on you to watch over their animals.

This can also be a wonderful part-time job for your children. If they have been asking for a pet and you are still undecided, suggest that they volunteer to pet sit so that they can prove their ability to keep a pet alive. They might surprise you with their level of commitment.

If your friends and neighbors do not have pets, volunteer to water their plants and take in the newspaper while they are gone. Demonstrate your commitment to the neighborhood by performing this service.

* *Assignment Whisper* *

April 22

Compliment a co-worker today.

It might work best to praise something that is related to the work they do. Let them know that you notice and appreciate their dedication to their job duties. Co-workers are more a part of your team than most people realize. Once you point out to them how their competence supports your duties, they might also begin to see how your abilities help them as well. It is a win/win for everyone involved.

If you feel comfortable, compliment them on something personal. This, however, could become complicated depending on the person and how closely you work with them. Be careful not to get too personal with someone you do not know well. Not everyone brings their private life to work with them.

If you are not employed outside the home, compliment your husband or kids for doing a chore around the house. Let them know how wonderful it is to see their commitment to the home team.

April 23

<u>Book recommendation</u>
Champagne for the Soul by Mike Mason is a life-changing book. It is written in a devotional format. Two pages a day for 90 days. It will transform your definition of "joy" and how you let it into your life. *Champagne for the Soul* teaches you about joy and how to be joyful no matter the circumstances. This is the book that will inspire your spirit every time you read it.

Mike Mason has written several other books that I enjoy. *The Gospel According to Job* walks through the book of Job verse by verse, exposing the text in a unique and thought-provoking way. You will never view the experiences of Job in the same way again.

Read *Champagne for the Soul* and commit yourself to leading a joyful life.

* *Assignment Whisper* *

April 24

Calling all artists!

Are you comfortable with a paint brush? Do you enjoy drawing or doodling? Do you see more than fifty unique shades of green when you take a springtime stroll in the park? If painting moves you, look for a canvas today.

If you enjoy painting pictures to hang on the wall, create something just for your church or office. Donate it for a springtime surprise.

If you enjoy murals, ask your church for permission to paint a mural on the nursery room wall. Ask your favorite restaurant if they would like a fresco in their lobby.

If you paint on glass, decorate a set of drinking glasses to donate to the break room of your local nursing home, hospital, or school.

If stamping is your passion, make a set of blank greeting cards to donate to soldiers. Our heroes in uniform always need cards to mail back home.

Whatever your talent, let your creative juices flow today. Fill a corner of the world with your artistic vision.

April 25

A Survival Kit for Everyday
Author Unknown

Toothpick - to remind you to pick out the good qualities in others ... Matt 7:1

Rubber band - to remind you to be flexible things might not always go the way you want, but it will work out....Romans 8:28

Band Aid - to remind you to heal hurt feelings, yours or someone else's ... Col 3:12-14

Pencil - To remind you to list your blessings everyday ... Ephesians 1:3

Eraser - to remind you that everyone makes mistakes, and it is okay ... Gen 50:15-21

Chewing gum - to remind you to stick with it and you can accomplish anything with Jesus ... Phil 4:13

Mint - to remind you that you are worth a mint to your heavenly father ... John 3:16-17

Candy Kiss - to remind you that everyone needs a kiss or a hug everyday ... 1 John 4:7

Tea Bag - to remind you to relax daily and go over that list of God's blessings ... 1 Thess 5:18

What do you need to survive? Do your survival tools complement your commitments in life?

* *Assignment Whisper* *

April 26

Include a cheerful note in your next mortgage payment or rent check.

Paying the mortgage or rent seldom produces entertainment. Money is tight. A large percentage of your mortgage payment goes to interest and escrow. The investment aspect of home ownership feels far removed from the monthly chore of writing the check.

If you pay a mortgage, you most likely write the check to a large bank or mortgage firm. The envelop is still opened by an individual. Write your cheerful note to the person who opens the envelop and processes your payment. Think of them opening their 200th envelop for the day and the joy they receive in discovering your note.

This note does not need to be earth-shaking or poetic. It simply needs to say that you remember that there are people involved in the process and acknowledge their commitment to their job.

* *Assignment Whisper* *

April 27

Today is toll road operator recognition day.

It is shocking to talk to toll booth operators and hear their stories of abuse. People routinely throw trash, swear, smash into their booths, and try to slip through without paying. Some drivers linger at the booth and leave their poor behavior before driving away.

Most people pay their toll and drive on past, having less than a minute's contact with the booth operator. Their indifference generates no smile for the operator. Faces are immediately forgotten.

Today, be the person that makes the day of the toll both operator. Be the person they tell their co-workers and families about as soon as they can. Make a sweet memory for these hard working folks.

Some ideas to put a smile on their faces include:

- ❖ Take cookies.
- ❖ Write a thank you note.
- ❖ Cut a bouquet of fresh flowers from your garden.
- ❖ Provide a CD of your favorite songs.
- ❖ Donate a bottle of hand lotion; handling money can dry skin quickly.
- ❖ Give them a magnet with an inspirational thought to decorate their booth.
- ❖ Furnish a disposable camera to take pictures of the nasty drivers' license plates!
- ❖ Note your ideas here.

* *Assignment Whisper* *

April 28

Today is parent appreciation day.

If you can, spend time with your parents today. Make a point to eliminate any distractions while you are together. Turn off you cell phone. Meet them in a place where you will not have distractions. Show them that you are committed to giving them your undivided attention. Even if they do not reciprocate the idea, you can still do it. If you speak to your parents on a regular basis, chances are that you do so with other things competing for your energy.

If your parents live far away, set aside some time to phone them when distractions are eliminated. You might want to phone them in the morning and arrange a time later in the day to chat without distractions.

If your parents are not living, write them a letter. Put in writing the things you would say if they were alive. Save this letter for your children when they are grown to give them a glimpse of the type of relationship you had with your parents. Preserve their memory and your relationship for the next generation.

Mother's Day comes in May. Father's Day follows in June. Grandparent's Day arrives in September. Today is different. Today honor your parents because you desire to be with them - not because the calendar dictates it.

* *Assignment Whisper* *

April 29

My dear brothers, take note of this: Everyone should be quick to listen, slow to speak and slow to become angry,

James 1:19

Quick to listen. We are all so good at that. Right? An amazing number of people believe themselves to be first-class listeners. Yet how many of us really are? Active listening is a learned behavior. It does not come naturally to most people.

Slow to speak. Most of us form our responses before the other person finishes their first sentence. We mentally encourage speakers to finish their thought faster as we wait simply *forever* for our turn to talk. Imagine what we would hear if we put our own thoughts on hold while someone was speaking to us.

Slow to become angry. Notice the flow of this one verse. It is common for anger to result from miscommunication. What is the primary cause of miscommunication? It is generally too much talking and not enough listening. Be quick to listen and slow to respond. Let the meaning sink into your brain before anger can be formed.

Pay attention to your anger today. When you find yourself becoming angry or even irritated, follow James' advice. Stop talking. Practice active listening to comprehend the true meaning of the conversation. Listen to what is actually being said before forming an opinion that might cause you to misunderstand.

* Assignment Whisper *

April 30

Today is fashion appreciation day.

Volunteer to help a friend who needs to find that perfect outfit for a special event. Maybe a senior high school student is looking for the perfect graduation dress. Perhaps their mother needs an outfit for the commencement ceremony.

If you are artistically inclined, spend the day volunteering at the local opera or theater guild sewing costumes for their next performance. Most productions have a costume designer, but an extra pair of hands always comes in handy (pun intended!)

Ask the local high school about their theater club. Are they preparing a play for the end of the year? If so, assist in their costume department.

If your community has a woman's shelter, lend a hand to their residents as they prepare for job interviews. Help the women sort through donations for clothing combinations that make them look their best. Boost their self-confidence with just the right outfit.

You do not have to be a clothing designer to be helpful. Even if you are not an avid reader of fashion magazines, you know when those shoes just do not complement that outfit. Even men know that leisure suits are outdated!

May 1

Today is Splendor Day.

When God created the earth, He included an incredible display of beauty in its design. More colors exist than can be counted. A variety of textures stimulate our need to touch from the day we are born. Sights, sounds, and smells were all created to provide pleasure and enjoyment.

God did not need to do that. The aerodynamic properties of birds do not rely on the color of their feathers. Humans need food to fuel their bodies regardless of how the aroma pleases our noses. How would my day be different if shrimp had smooth skin?

There are, however, some practical reasons for colors, textures, and smells. Flowers use their colors to attract bees for pollination. Animals employ their scents for mating. Porcupines apply their body's unique texture for protection from predators. God had reasons for creating things the way that He did even when they are not obvious to us.

Take some time today to enjoy the splendor of God's creation. Notice the colors and smells. Enjoy a walk in the park and rejoice in the new life that arrives each spring. See the world as God's canvas. Appreciate the beauty that He incorporated in everything He made.

May 2

Today, enjoy the beauty of your spouse.

Have your picture taken with your spouse today because he is so handsome or she is so lovely. This does not need to be a formal portrait. Have fun with the idea. Get your kids involved. Have them snap some candid photos of you together.

When you view the photos, remember to tell your spouse how beautiful he or she is in your eyes. Express to your mate how proud you are to be his or her spouse. Let your sweetheart know that you love him or her - their beauty, wrinkles, and the whole package.

Find a nice frame for your favorite picture. Ask your children to make one for you. If you are crafty in any way, make a frame that reflects your talents. Let the photo and the frame show guests in your home who you are.

Formal portraits are also nice to have. If it has been some time since your last formal portrait, consider doing that today as well. Use them as Mother's Day and Father's Day gifts, too.

If you are not married, have your picture taken with a relative or close friend instead.

May 3

Today continues yesterday's photo shoot theme.

Have your picture taken with each of your children individually. Tell them that you want the photos because you are proud of the lovely people they have become. Let them know that you think they are beautiful on the outside as well as the inside. Build their self image throughout the day.

If you included your kids in the formal sitting with your spouse yesterday, spend today taking candid shots of you and your spouse with your kids. With digital photography, this is an inexpensive activity to do. Copy the photos onto CD and put one in each child's baby book. Keep the memories alive!

If you do not have children, have your photo taken with nieces and nephews today. Share these photos with other family members.

May 4

Give your yard a face lift today.

Decorate your yard or front door area. Make the entrance to your house look inviting and friendly. Visitors will appreciate this, but you will, too. Think how fun it is to come home to a pretty space!

Ideas to dress your front door include:

❖Buy a potted plant.
❖Paint your door a new color.
❖Hang a decoration on the door.
❖Get creative with the door knocker.

Some other ideas include:

❖Plant fresh flowers.
❖Trim the hedges.
❖Refresh the mulch.
❖Install a new ring tone to your doorbell.
❖Clean the patio furniture.
❖Buy new chair cushions for the patio furniture.
❖Paint or repair areas near your primary entrance.
❖Install a motion-activated light over your door.

Spring is the time to make things new. Take this opportunity to infuse springtime splendor into your home.

May 5

Remember your hair stylist today.

It is not as easy as it might seem to be a hair stylist. Imagine standing on a hard floor listening to people complain all day. People often confuse the beauty salon with a therapist office, telling their stylist all the troubling events of their lives.

Hair stylists are also under pressure to give you the perfect service. Just think what a terrible day for a hair stylists looks like. All of their customers would qualify for the "Bad Hair Day" award! If they make a mistake, there is little that can be done to repair it.

Here are some ideas to brighten their day:

- ❖ Donate fabric softener sheets. Lots of towels are washed in salons.
- ❖ Decorate a broom with the shop's name on it.
- ❖ Take cookies.
- ❖ Write a thank you note. Deliver it in person or put it in the mail.
- ❖ Cut a bouquet of fresh flowers from your garden.
- ❖ Donate a bottle of hand lotion for after the long hours their hands spend in water.
- ❖ Order pizza delivered for lunch.
- ❖ Note your ideas here.

May 6

Help beautify your community today.

Volunteer at Habitat for Humanity. Their website explains the history of this organization as follows: "Jimmy Carter put Habitat for Humanity on the map. This international organization was founded in 1976 by Millard Fuller along with his wife, Linda. Since that time, they have built nearly 300,000 houses around the world, providing more than 1.5 million people in more than 3,000 communities with safe, decent, affordable shelter. They do not require any construction experience or expertise. They will provide on-the-job training for volunteers who wish to help build homes and futures."

Habitat has numerous other ways to support their cause. Fundraising, advertising, mentoring families, and stuffing envelopes are just a few ways to serve this organization. Visit www.habitat.org for more information.

Rebuild Together is a similar organization. Rebuild Together does not build homes from the ground up. This group focuses on repairing and maintaining existing homes for seniors, disabled people, veterans, and people displaced by natural disasters. Learn more about this organization by visiting www.rebuildingtogether.org.

Many communities and churches have local groups that offer these same sorts of activities. Check with your church's leaders or community center staff for information on projects in your city.

* *Assignment Whisper* *

May 7

Do you have a passion for horses? Visit http://www.adoptafoal.org to gather ideas about involvement in animal rescue. More than likely your part of the nation has a similar organization.

Animals need rescuing for many different reasons. Perhaps there was a flood or hurricane that left them stranded. Sometimes owners relocate and cannot take the animals with them. Maybe there was a death in the family limiting the care that the animals received. Whatever the case may be, there are numerous ways for animal lovers to volunteer their talents.

If you are able to travel, spend some time today researching organizations that provide animal rescue to areas impacted by natural disasters. Contact these organizations today so that you are prepared when the need arises.

May 8

Today is sharing day.

Spend some time today thinking over the year, your whispering experiences, and how it has impacted your life. Share these thoughts with a friend. Present them with a copy of this book so that they can also begin whispering. Invite them to join you in this assignment.

As previously mentioned, people are so often willing to do the ideas presented here, but they frequently need help getting started. Help a friend begin their own whispering today. Share the joy that this book has brought to you.

Your friend's favorite activities might take you out of your comfort zone farther than you would like. It is OK. Flow with it for just one day. Later you can take your friends outside of their comfort zone, too. Create beauty by trying new things today.

* *Assignment Whisper* *

May 9

Volunteer with Mothers Against Drunk Driving.

Since 1980, MADD's mission has been: "to stop drunk driving, support the victims of this violent crime and prevent underage drinking."

The volunteer needs of this organization are varied. You could help stuff envelopes or organize a fundraiser. Providing accounting expertise or developing a website are also options. If you are bilingual, volunteer to translate for them.

This organization can use volunteers who can commit to regular hours as well as those who only have a couple of hours a year to spare. Some opportunities are temporary; others are ongoing.

Visit www.madd.org for more information.

May 10

The Quilt
Author Unknown

As I faced my Maker at the last judgment, I knelt before the Lord along with all the other souls.

Before each of us laid our lives like the squares of a quilt in many piles. An Angel sat before each of us sewing our quilt squares together into a tapestry that is our life. But as my angel took each piece of cloth off the pile, I noticed how ragged and empty each of my squares was. They were filled with giant holes. Each square was labeled with a part of my life that had been difficult, the challenges and temptations I was faced with in everyday life. I saw hardships that I endured, which were the largest holes of all.

I glanced around me. Nobody else had such squares. Other than a tiny hole here and there, the other tapestries were filled with rich color and the bright hues of worldly fortune. I gazed upon my own life and was disheartened. My angel was sewing the ragged pieces of cloth together, threadbare and empty, like binding air.

Finally the time came when each life was to be displayed, held up to the light, the scrutiny of truth. The others rose, each in turn, holding up their tapestries. So filled their lives had been. My angel looked upon me, and nodded for me to rise. My gaze dropped to the ground in shame. I had not had all the earthly fortunes. I had love in my life, and laughter. But there had also been trials of illness, and death, and false accusations that took from me my world, as I knew it. I had to start over many times.

* *Assignment Whisper* *

I often struggled with the temptation to quit, only to somehow muster the strength to pick up and begin again. I spent many nights on my knees in prayer, asking for help and guidance in my life. I had often been held up to ridicule, which I endured painfully, each time offering it up to the Father in hopes that I would not melt within my skin beneath the judgmental gaze of those who unfairly judged me.

And now, I had to face the truth. My life was what it was, and I had to accept it for what it was. I rose and slowly lifted the combined squares of my life to the light. An awe-filled gasp filled the air. I gazed around at the others who stared at me with wide eyes. Then, I looked upon the tapestry before me Light flooded the many holes, creating an image, the face of Christ. Then our Lord stood before me, with warmth and love in His eyes. He said, "Every time you gave over your life to Me, it became My life, My hardships, and My struggles. Each point of light in your life is when you stepped aside and let Me shine through, until there was more of Me than there was of you." May all our quilts be threadbare and worn, allowing Christ to shine through.

What blocked your view today? Did you obstruct someone else's view today? Did you let God's beauty shine through your actions?

* _Assignment Whisper_ *

May 11

Thank the bus boy at your favorite restaurant today.

Clearing tables is not a fun job. Rude patrons will sometimes leave messes on purpose to be mean to the bus boy. Even customers who are neat and respective still leave their dinner for someone else to clear. The table has to be clean and ready for the next customer. It's a dirty job, but someone has to do it (as they say.)

Is the bus boy a teen? Think about what this teen would rather be doing than clearing your table. He or she would probably rather be hanging out with friends, taking their boyfriend or girlfriend on a date, spending time with their family, or working a job that is more fulfilling than bussing tables. Help this teenager to have a good day at work by thanking them for their dedication to their job.

Is the bus boy an adult? Give some thought to the circumstances that caused this person to apply for a job as a bus boy. Most adults I know would not appreciate a job that pays minimum wage to do such a menial task. You do not have to know the details of their life story to show them appreciation and respect.

Remember to pray for these people, too. They will be blessed by your prayers.

May 12

Recognize your travel agent today.

Economic times are tough as this book goes to press. Being a travel agent is about as lucrative as being a real estate agent right now, and that is not saying much. When money is tight, people do not travel. Those who can afford to travel are visiting relatives more often that taking trips to Europe. Being a travel agent can be a lonely job when the economy is bad.

Here are some ideas to brighten their day:

❖ Take cookies.
❖ Write a thank you note. Deliver it in person or put it in the mail.
❖ Cut a bouquet of fresh flowers from your garden.
❖ Sing cheerful songs with your children.
❖ Donate a bottle of hand lotion; handling paperwork all day can dry skin.
❖ Order pizza delivered for lunch.
❖ Note your ideas here.

May 13

A second grader came home from school and said to her mother, "Mom, guess what? We learned how to make babies today."

The mother, more than a little surprised, tried to keep her cool.

"That is interesting," she said, "How do you make babies?"

"It's simple," replied the girl. "You just change "y" to "i" and add 'es'."

Did you misunderstand someone today? Make a point to listen to people as they speak to you. Discipline yourself to keep cool until you know what the other person is saying.

Did someone else misunderstand you today? Give some thought to how you communicate with others to avoid misunderstandings in the future.

Effective communication skills eliminate all sorts of negative emotions. Anger, frustration, and fear often follow miscommunication. When people truly understand each other, the world is far more beautiful place.

* *Assignment Whisper* *

May 14

Thank the security people at your local mall today.

The security people at the mall have a thankless and often boring job. Some people see them as "pretend police." Other people see them as a threat. Mothers often hope they will act as babysitters or enforcers. Most of them have family at home missing them.

In larger cities, security jobs are often a second job for regular police officers. They are a reminder that police are not paid enough to be on the receiving end of a burglar's pistol. Some officers are paid less than a professional football player's travel expenses for a season.

Security guards do not get much respect, or much sleep. Go out of your way to day to thank them. Remind them that they are appreciated and valued.

May 15

Empowerment. People of all ages like to feel that they are empowered. Most people have had a job that involves responsibility without the authority necessary to accomplish the task. It is not a pleasant position to be in regardless of the circumstances.

Today find the opportunity to empower someone or remind someone that they are empowered. This might be as simple as trusting your child with a new assignment. Let them use the stove for the first time or drive the car in the driveway. It may be more complex, such as assigning new duties to a subordinate at work. Discover or create a situation that makes someone else feel empowered today.

Visit www.loveourchildrenusa.org for some ideas. Their goal is this:

"Love Our Children USA works to eliminate behaviors that keep children from reaching their potential. It redefines parenting and creates kid success by promoting prevention strategies and positive changes in parenting and family attitudes and behaviors through public education. Love Our Children USA honors and respects children and works to empower and support children, teens, parents and families through information, resources, advocacy, and online youth mentoring. Its goal is to keep children safe and strengthen families - Its message is positive... one of prevention, empowerment and hope."

May 16

Go therefore and make disciples of all the nations, baptizing them in the name of the Father and the Son and the Holy Spirit, teaching them to observe all that I commanded you; and lo, I am with you always, even to the end of the age.

Matthew 28:19-20

Before departing, Jesus made it clear to his disciples what they were to do next. Make disciples of all the nations. Teach them to observe God's commandments. For Christians, this is our goal, our calling, our purpose. With all that we do, all that we say, and all that we support, we are projecting Christ's character to the world.

Therefore, it is important to watch what we are doing, saying, and promoting. Do our actions toward others reflect the desires of our hearts? Do they verify our cause, or would others say that they do not know our heart?

Spend some time today reflecting on whether people know who you are in your heart. If they know you as something other than how you see yourself, how can you change your behavior so that it projects your true heart?

St. Francis of Assisi summed it up like this, "Preach the Gospel always, and when necessary use words."

* *Assignment Whisper* *

May 17

Donate to your local thrift store today. Countless people depend on donations to survive. It can appear that the store's inventory is overwhelming. However, their supply has an amazing turnover rate as well. Help the thrift store recipients by donating what you can. Even if you only have one or two things that you no longer need, that contribution is appreciated.

If you have time, volunteer at the local thrift shop. This is a good time of year to volunteer as the summer is approaching. Many families with children will be shopping for school clothes and other things in the coming months. Plan now to donate your time to help the thrift store prepare.

Thrift store volunteers help sort clothing, clean the show room, display sale items, assist families in finding what they need, provide clerical services, and recruit more volunteers. It is also important that the shoppers feel welcome in the store. Put on your best smile and greet them at the door. You would be astonished what a difference that can make.

* *Assignment Whisper* *

May 18

Encourage your employer to sponsor a charitable organization or event.

With the holiday season long past and summer schedules not yet applied, this is the perfect time to promote the idea of charity.

If your employer already has a cause that they support, volunteer to be more active in their efforts. Organize a new type of fundraiser. Promote the activities to your co-workers. Ensure that new employees are aware of the cause. Make posters for the employee lounge. Create a screen saver for your computer that advertises the cause or events. Before you know it, everyone will be caught up in your enthusiasm.

If your place of employment does not already have a cause, suggest one. Do your research ahead of time. Use www.charitynavigator.org to gather information to support your idea. Develop a plan with enough details to demonstrate your sincerity.

* *Assignment Whisper* *

May 19

Volunteer at your local Red Cross today.

People often have misconception about the work of the Red Cross. Medical background or experience is not required. You do not need to wait for a huge natural disaster that impacts a large geographic region. Did you know that the Red Cross responses to 150 home fires every day?

The Red Cross also provides educational classes throughout the year. Babysitting, CPR, swimming, health, and safety classes are just a few of the classes conducted by Red Cross volunteers across the globe. Other volunteers assist with training and organizing volunteer staff. Red Cross volunteers also deliver emergency messages between family members of the armed services. Regardless of the amount of time you have to donate, you could make a huge difference in someone's life by volunteering your time to the Red Cross in your area.

For more information, visit their website at www.redcross.org.

May 20

Volunteer at the local Alzheimer's Association or nursing home that specializes in Alzheimer's care. According to the Alzheimer information website, as many as 5.2 million people in the United States alone are living with this disease. Alzheimer's is currently the sixth leading cause of death.

Volunteer activities are countless. A few ideas include:

❖Assist people with making their homes safe.

❖Have tea with a caregiver of an Alzheimer's patient.

❖Babysit a patient so that the caregiver can have some time to themselves.

❖Donate puzzles or movies to an Alzheimer's center.

❖Provide telephone support or clerical assistance at a center.

❖Play the piano to entertain the residents.

❖Bake cookies for the staff and residents.

For more ideas or locations of local chapters, visit www.alz.org.

May 21

But if any of you lacks wisdom, let him ask of God, who gives to all men generously and without reproach, and it will be given to him. But let him ask in faith without any doubting, for the one who doubts is like the surf of the sea driven and tossed by the wind.

James 1:5-6

Are you feeling as if you have yet to find the one volunteer opportunity that makes your heart sing? Are you frustrated or feel tossed in the wind with regard to where and how you should be sharing yourself?

Do not be discouraged. James reminded us that there is a way to receive wisdom. You have only to ask God in faith. He will not only provide you wisdom but will do so generously.

Perhaps you are feeling like you found your calling but that calling turned out to be a big surprise. You were expecting something else, but look where you are now! Rest assured, my friend, that it was no surprise to God. You are exactly where He wants you to be, doing what He needs you to do. Remember that we do not always see the big picture in the same way God does. He can see the impact of our actions far better than we ever could. Continue to follow His lead in faith. Know that His wisdom and guidance are there for the asking and only a pray away.

* *Assignment Whisper* *

May 22

Volunteer at your local radio station today.

Many areas of the country have several stations. Choose your favorite and ask how you can volunteer. You will probably get a tour behind the scenes and meet some fascinating people in the process.

There are many facets of a radio station's operations that most people do not consider. Without the visual aspect of advertising, a creative spirit is required. Many stations interview guests who may have no experience in radio and need some coaching. If you have skill in this area, volunteering at a radio station might be just your cup of tea.

Consider what it is like to work at a radio station with no real-time interaction with an audience. The microphone is your only audience. It takes a special skill to continue to sound personal and enthusiastic when there is no face to make a connection. Let these people know that you are listening and appreciate their work.

Some ideas to contribute to radio station needs include:

❖Providing clerical assistance.
❖Decorate their reception area.
❖Search the internet for news items.
❖Screen calls.
❖Develop fundraising activities.
❖Design websites.
❖Note your ideas here.

May 23

If you are to this point in the year and still feel as though you are operating inside your comfort zone, I would like to recommend a book to you. Pick up a copy of *If You Want to Walk on Water, You've Got to Get Out of the Boat* by John Ortberg.

Mr. Ortberg lays out very clearly and comically why it is important to venture beyond our comfort zones when serving God. His stories and insights will both entertain you and challenge you. You will also feel empowered as you are reminded how God will sustain you outside your comfort zone as well as inside your safe place.

While some days of this devotional may prove effortless, other days require more energy. If you have been ignoring those days, I encourage you to rethink that strategy. Select one thing that felt outside your comfort zone and try it today.

Note your ventures into foreign waters here. Check back at the end of the year to see if it still feels outside of your comfort zone.

* *Assignment Whisper* *

May 24

Volunteer at a museum today.

Have you ever wondered who dusts the displays in the museum? Who waters the plants? Are you curious who mails the flyers to your house? Who decides what exhibits will arrive next year? These are just some of the areas that volunteers organize at museums.

If you have museums in your area, contact the local board for more information on volunteer opportunities. Like many other places, some tasks require regular commitment while others may be seasonal or temporary in nature. Perhaps you have specialized talents that would benefit a current or future exhibit, or maybe you are more skilled at stuffing envelopes. Either way, the museum can use your time and energy.

If you do not have a museum in your area, contact your local chapter of the historical society. They may not have an office or physical location, but chances are high that someone in your area is dedicated to preserving the region's history. You can meet some amazing people this way. Who knows? You might even meet a relative that you never knew you had!

* *Assignment Whisper* *

May 25

Do something for a sibling today.

Some people are blessed with wonderful families. They maintain close connections with their siblings throughout the year. Their brothers/sisters know everything that is happening in their lives. If this is your family, count your blessings today. Call each of your brothers and sisters and tell them how much it means to you that they are in your life.

If you have a sibling who has been asking you for something specific that you repeatedly reschedule, do that activity with him or her today. Do not take this sibling for granted. Appreciate his or her involvement in your life.

If you are an only child, think of that one friend who has felt like a sibling to you. Most everyone has a friend who has been with them through thick and thin. Call that person today or arrange to spend some time with him or her as soon as possible. Make this a special time, a day that is a memory forever. Give it 100% of your attention.

If you have siblings but are not close to them, use today to being the process of creating new memories with your brothers and sisters. Chat with them on the phone. Invite them over for dinner. The goal is not to rehash old hurts or revive old pains. The purpose is to start the baby steps of developing a new relationship with your siblings. Like they say, there's no time like the present!

* Assignment Whisper *

May 26

Write a thank you note to an ambassador today.

Do you know how many ambassadors there are in the United States alone? Have you ever wondered how many Americans serve as ambassadors to other nations or to the United Nations? The number might surprise you. Some nations have more than one embassy in the United States.

For a complete list of ambassadors currently serving in the United States, visit this website: www.state.gov/s/cpr/c23721.htm.

For information on Americans serving as ambassadors to other nations, this website has more information. Visit this link: www.americanambassadors.org.

If you are interested in the United Nations, visit www.usunnewyork.usmission.gov.

Volunteering for an ambassador or in an embassy may take more coordination than other volunteer opportunities. Security issues must be addressed. If this is of interest to you, start researching the idea now. Writing a thank you note might be a good way to introduce yourself.

* *Assignment Whisper* *

May 27

In happy moments--praise God.
In difficult moments--seek God.
In quiet moments--worship God.
In painful moments--trust God.
Every moment--thank God.

This is a common saying that most people have seen or heard at some point in their lives. Perhaps you have seen it on a t-shirt or a memo pad. It might be on your mouse pad or a poster at church. It is familiar to many of us.

Today spend some time absorbing its meaning. Note that no matter the circumstances, God remains at the end. He is present no matter what happens. He is the ultimate goal of all of our endeavors.

Use this poem to remind yourself that all of your "whispering" is for God. Each suggestion in this devotional is designed to draw you closer to God by serving others.

If serving others causes happiness, praise God. When whispering is difficult, seek God. When whispering through quiet prayer and meditation, worship God. If whispering revives old pains, trust God. In every whispering moment, thank God for all things.

May 28

Volunteer at a local parks and recreation facility.

If your city supports a large parks and recreation department, finding volunteer opportunities will be easy. They are probably in the process of finalizing summer schedules of camps and classes. Volunteer to assist, teach, organize, or advertise these activities. Skill or knowledge of plants and local foliage is not necessarily required. If you do not know the difference between a weed and a rose, do not let this stop you from volunteering in this area. There are many other projects that parks need volunteer energies to complete.

If you live in a rural area that does not have a parks department, volunteer to pick up litter at the local park or cemetery. Adopting a stretch of road to remove debris. Help make your area more beautiful as summer arrives.

May 29

Volunteer to be a stage hand at local theater group or orchestra.

An extra pair of hands is always a benefit when the curtain is raised. Costumes need adjustments. Make up needs refreshing. Sets need changing. Actors might need prompting or help with costume changes between scenes. If the theater group is small, other actors probably perform these tasks. They can always use the help.

If you have never watched a play from back stage, you will be amazed how much fun it can be. By volunteering to work, you will also be attending the production. Take a friend with you and make a night of it. Dinner and a show for the price of dinner alone!

Years ago, I volunteered for a small theater group. My job was to hand out programs prior to the show and pick up the programs left in the theater at the end of the show. For approximately 30 minutes of work, I received approximately two hours of entertainment. It was a good trade to me.

* *Assignment Whisper* *

May 30

Did you know that in 2007, 60.8 million volunteers performed 8.1 billion hours of service? This is according to the website-
www.volunteeringinamerica.gov.
This website has useful information on a wide variety of topics concerning volunteering.

Do you know what "voluntourism" means? It is the idea of long distance volunteerism. Each year more and more people volunteer in areas far from their homes. In response to hurricanes in the Gulf Coast and fires in California, people from around the country drove supplies to those in need. Doctors without Borders volunteers visit countries in need of specialized services.

New organizations grow from the desire of people who want to use their vacation time helping others. If this idea interests you, check out www.globalvolunteers.org for information.

Start a new family tradition of volunteering each year instead of spending spring break on the beach.

If you were thinking that you had to pass on your summer vacation this year to continue "whispering," think again. You can take a vacation and "whisper" through the whole thing!

May 31

Volunteer at an assisted living center today.

Many residents of assisted living centers are independent, yet unable to drive. They may need to run some errands, do some shopping, or just have lunch at the new restaurant in town. Whatever the case, spend some time today with a resident of an assisted living center.

As I grow older, I notice that more and more of my elderly friends need help addressing their Christmas cards each year. Imagine how much joy you could bring to people by writing letters for people who can no longer do that task themselves. Many people in assisted living residences are on fixed and low incomes. Phone calls to relatives may be outside their budget. Letters may be physically difficult to write. Help them keep in contact with their friends and family by being their hands.

If you have a cell phone service with unlimited long distance calling, allow someone to use your phone for a brief call or two. The staff at the center could help you identify which residents would benefit the most from this sort of generosity.

* *Assignment Whisper* *

June 1

Have you ever felt at a loss when it comes to prayer? Do you sometimes feel like you just do not have the hang of it? You are not alone. Even the disciples, the men closest to Jesus, asked for instructions in this area.

Open your Bible with me to Luke chapter 11. The first verse in this chapter reads:

And it came about that while He was praying in a certain place, after He had finished, one of His disciples said to Him, "Lord, teach us to pray just as John [the Baptist] taught his disciples."

Jesus answers the question with this response (verses 2-4):

And He said to them, "When you pray, say: Father, hallowed by Thy name. Thy kingdom come. Give us each day our daily bread. And forgive us our sins, For we ourselves also forgive everyone who is indebted to us. And lead us not into temptation."

Many wonderful books cover the topic of prayer. I like Jesus' instructions the best, however. When in doubt, go to the source.

In my opinion, the most important thing to remember about prayer is that it is a conversation with a friend. Jesus wants a personal relationship with you. Talk to him in the same way that you converse to a trusted friend.

Spend time today eliminating your discomfort with prayer. It is not as difficult as we often make it out to be.

June 2

Yesterday you had a prayerful conversation with Jesus. Today is your spouse's turn.

Set aside significant time today to listen to your spouse with 100% of your soul. Eliminate *every* interruption. Turn off the phone (cell phones, too.) Unplug your computer. Disconnect yourself completely from the electronic toys that feel so urgent. Turn off the radio and television, too.

Put the kids on notice that you are having some adult time that is not to be interrupted. Hire a babysitter if necessary. If you have an older child, hire them to entertain the younger children.

And most importantly, put aside everything disturbing your mind. Leave your unfinished "to do" list on your desk. Forget about everything that has to be accomplished tomorrow. The only thing that should be in your mind is what is coming out of your spouse's mouth. Give him or her 100% of your attention in every respect.

Please note that I am not advocating a therapy session here. This time is not about solving the problems of the world. It does not need to be productive or inspired. Talk about the weather or the new movie that opened this weekend. Whatever the topic, the idea is to listen with your whole being.

Your life is happening now. Be present for it.

June 3

The focus of today is a continuation of yesterday. Apply yesterday's concept to your children.

If you have more than one child, make every effort to spend quality time with each child individually today. Depending on the ages and stages of your children, this might last one minute to one hour. Make quality your goal - not quantity.

If your kids are at the age when they do not have time for their parents, force the issue. Remember when they were toddlers and did not want to sit still? Remember teaching them how to sit for one minute, then two, etc., until they could last through an entire meal? Use that technique again to teach them to talk to you.

If your children are grown and have homes of their own, call them or invite them to lunch. Remember that the goal is to have no distractions whatsoever so that you can listen as attentively as possible. If they do not want to talk about personal things, do not let it concern you. Do everything you can to just listen and let them do the talking. Make every attempt to refrain from making comments that sound as if you are judging their life choices.

If you do not have children, contact a niece or nephew or other relative for this day's whisper.

Assignment Whisper *

June 4

Send a thank you note to college professors. Thank them for their dedication to the profession.

Perhaps you remember a special teacher from college. If this person is still teaching, write to him or her and describe how he or she shaped who you have become. Be specific regarding how the teaching methods or subject matter impacted your life. Encourage this professor to continue those traits that you remember as uplifting.

If you never went to college or feel it was too long ago, browse the internet site of your local campus to pick a professor. You might end up taking a class from this teacher one day!

If you have children in school, write a thank you note to their teachers. Tell them some of the nice things that your children say about them at home. Teachers are often caught between following the rules of the administration and doing what works best for the child. It takes a special person to teach a large group of kids in an organization that is ultimately controlled by the federal government.

It might also be a good idea to check your spelling and grammar in your note!

* *Assignment Whisper* *

June 5

Consider the definition of "prayer" today.

Webster's dictionary defines prayer as "the act or practice of praying to God or a god." This is not particularly helpful in developing a prayer life.

The Bible defines prayer as seeking, asking, or entreating to God. In the New Testament, the idea of an interview is also included in the definition of prayer. There is a "coming together" or a "visit" between the parties involved with prayer.

This definition is much more helpful to me. The vision of coming together to visit each other is something most people enjoy. It is as if you are saying to Jesus, "Let's get some coffee," or "Come over for a chat." Invite Jesus over to scrapbook with you or go for a bike ride on a sunny summer day.

How do you define prayer? Is it a definition that is comfortable for you? Does it move your heart or make you weary? Does it function in all situations of your life? Is it something easily modeled to your children and friends? If not, spend today making some adjustments to your definition and practice of prayer.

June 6

Volunteer at your local zoo.

Do not worry! I am not suggesting that you feed raw meat to the lion family. There are many other ways to volunteer at your local zoo.

Some suggestions include:

❖Fundraising.

❖Coordinating field trips with school groups.

❖Advertising.

❖Providing clerical support.

❖Assisting in the gift shop.

❖Handling assistant trainer duties.

❖Serving as the parking lot attendant.

❖Offering accounting and bookkeeping help.

❖Editing or managing advertising.

If you do not have a zoo in your area, write a thank you note to the zoo nearest your home. The zoo provides a wonderful service to the residents it serves. Let the staff know that you appreciate the things they do and the service they provide to the community.

June 7

The Bat, Buzzard and Bumblebee
Author Unknown

If you put a buzzard in a pen six or eight feet square and entirely open at the top, the bird, in spite of his ability to fly, will be an absolute prisoner. The reason is that a buzzard always begins a flight from the ground with a run of ten or twelve feet. Without space to run, as is his habit, he will not even attempt to fly, but will remain a prisoner for life in a small jail with no top.

The ordinary bat that flies around at night, a remarkable nimble creature in the air, cannot take off from a level place. If it is placed on the floor or flat ground, all it can do is shuffle about helplessly and, no doubt, painfully, until it reaches some slight elevation from which it can throw itself into the air. Then, at once, it takes off like a flash.

A bumblebee, if dropped into an open tumbler will be there until it dies unless it is taken out. It never sees the means of escape at the top, but persists in trying to find some way out through the sides near the bottom. It will seek a way where none exists, until it completely destroys itself.

In many ways, there are lots of people like the buzzard, the bat and the bee. They are struggling about with all their problems and frustrations, not realizing that if they look up, they will find the answer.

Where are you looking?

June 8

If baking is your passion, today will be a fun day for you. Let me introduce you to the Baking GALS.

Their purpose as stated on their website is: "Baking GALS (GALS stands for Give A Little Support) is a group of volunteer bakers who bake and ship homemade goodies to our heroic troops that are currently deployed. Each soldier is "Hosted" by a blogger, and potential bakers are "recruited" from the bloggers own site as well as the GALS site. Each Host recruits between 20-25 bakers, meaning LOTS of goodies get delivered to our soldier...so many, in fact that he or she has plenty to share with their fellow troops!"

Gather your friends and exchange a few recipes. The soldiers are probably missing home and the summer activities that they would be enjoying if they were not deployed. Nothing says "home" like a batch of homemade cookies. Since you will need taste testers before shipping the cookies, this is a fun way to host a summer party and send some cheer as well.

With the kids out of school, they can help with the baking, too. If boredom has set in already, the smell of freshly baked cookies will revive the kids.

Visit www.bakinggals.com for more information.

* *Assignment Whisper* *

June 9

While attending a Marriage Seminar dealing with communication, Tom and his wife, Grace, listened to the instructor.

"It is essential that husbands and wives know each other's likes and dislikes."

He addressed the man, "Can you name your wife's favorite flower?"

Tom leaned over, touched his wife's arm gently and whispered, "It's Pillsbury, isn't it?

While you probably chuckled over this joke, chances are that you also related to the punch line. We have all had times when we felt that those close to us have completely missed the point of something that was important to us.

Spend some time today thinking about the "Pillsbury" moments in your life. Who have you misunderstood, and what was the impact of that? How can you make amends? How can you change your listening habits and social cues to avoid these situations in the future? Who in your life would say this joke reminds them of you?

Think what a service it would be to your friends and family if you never caused misunderstandings like this.

* *Assignment Whisper* *

June 10

Today is neighbor day.

How many more neighbors do you have to meet before the National Night Out in August? Can you accomplish this goal if you do not engage in today's whispering assignment? There is still time to reach that goal.

Is there a particular neighbor that you have avoided? Tackle that neighbor today. Invite them over for tea. Welcome their children to play in the sprinkler. Deliver a plate of cookies and tell them about the Baking GALS idea. Even if you only spend ten minutes with this neighbor, use today to break the ice.

June 11

<u>Five Fingers of Prayer</u>
Author Unknown

1. Your thumb is nearest to you. So begin your prayers by praying for those closest to you. They are the easiest to remember. To pray for our loved ones is, as C.S. Lewis once said, a "sweet duty."

2. The next finger is the pointing finger. Pray for those who teach, instruct and heal. This includes teachers, nurses, doctors, and ministers. They need support and wisdom in pointing others in the right direction. Keep them in your prayers.

3. The next finger is the tallest finger. It reminds us of our leaders. Pray for the president, leaders in business and industry, and administrators. These people shape our nation and guide public opinion. They need God's guidance.

4. The fourth finger is our ring finger. Surprising to many is the fact that this is our weakest finger; as any piano teacher will testify. It should remind us to pray for those who are weak, in trouble or in pain. They need your prayers day and night. You cannot pray too much for them.

5. Lastly comes our little finger; the smallest finger of all. Which is where we should place ourselves in relation to God and others. As the Bible says, "The least shall be the greatest among you." Your pinkie should remind you to pray for yourself. By the time you have prayed for the other four groups, your own needs will be put into proper perspective and you will be able to pray for yourself more effectively.

June 12

The ABC'S of Friendship
Author Unknown

A lways be honest, would you want THEM to lie to you?
B e there when they need you, or you may wind up alone.
C heer them on, we all need encouragement now and then.
D o not look for their faults, even if you have none.
E ncourage their dreams, what would we be without them?
F orgive them, you just MAY do something wrong sometime.
G et together often, misery loves company, so does glee.
H ave faith in them, the human animal is remarkable.
I nclude them, you may need to be included sometime.
J ust be there when they need you.
K now when they need a hug, and couldn't you use one?
L ove them unconditionally, that is the ONLY condition.
M ake them feel special, because aren't we ALL special?
N ever forget them, who wants to feel forgotten?
O ffer to help, and know when "No thanks" is just politeness.
P raise them honestly and openly.
Q uietly disagree, noisy NO's make enemies.
R eally listen, a friendly ear is a soothing balm.
S ay you are sorry, do not let them assume it.
T alk frequently, communication is important.
U se good judgment.
V erbalize your feelings!
W ish them luck, hopefully good!
X amine your motives before you "help" out.
Y our words count, use them wisely.
Z ip your lips when told a secret.

* *Assignment Whisper* *

June 13

Volunteer with an organization that supports brain injuries.

If you have ever met anyone who has a child with any sort of brain disorder, you will have some understanding of how isolated these people may feel. They are not always able to take their children to places that most parents frequent. If they have other children who developed normally, they may miss some of their favorite activities because their sibling cannot attend. Coping with the social, emotional, and medical needs can be exhausting for everyone involved.

If you know someone who has a child with special needs, remember to invite them to events when you can. If you are a parent, you will know that all kids need patience and compassion in certain situations. Make the effort to include those kids who need a tad more patience than your children. Include the parents as well.

There are many agencies across the globe that support people with brain disorders as well as their families. Here are a few suggestions:

❖www.liliclairefoundation.org
❖www.bianh.org
❖www.marchofdimes.com
❖www.nodcc.org
❖www.rarediseases.org

June 14

Daddy's Empty Chair
Author Unknown

A man's daughter had asked the local minister to come and pray with her father. When the minister arrived, he found the man lying in bed with his head propped up on two pillows. An empty chair sat beside his bed. The minister assumed that the old fellow had been informed of his visit.

"I guess you were expecting me, he said.

"No, who are you?" said the father.

The minister told him his name and then remarked, "I saw the empty chair, and I figured you knew I was going to show up,"

"Oh yeah, the chair," said the bedridden man. "Would you mind closing the door?"

Puzzled, the minister shut the door.

"I have never told anyone this, not even my daughter," said the man. "But all of my life I have never known how to pray. At church I used to hear the pastor talk about prayer, but it went right over my head. I abandoned any attempt at prayer," the old man continued, "until one day four years ago, my best friend said to me, 'Johnny, prayer is just a simple matter of having a conversation with Jesus. Here is what I suggest. Sit down in a chair; place an empty chair in front of you, and in faith see Jesus on the chair. It is not spooky because he promised, 'I will be with you always'. Then just speak to him in the same way you are doing with me right now."

"So, I tried it and I have liked it so much that I do it a couple of hours every day. I am careful though. If my daughter saw me talking to an empty chair, she would either have a nervous breakdown or send me off to the funny farm."

* *Assignment Whisper* *

The minister was deeply moved by the story and encouraged the old man to continue on the journey. Then he prayed with him, anointed him with oil, and returned to the church.

Two nights later the daughter called to tell the minister that her daddy had died that afternoon.

"Did he die in peace?" he asked.

Yes, when I left the house about two o'clock, he called me over to his bedside, told me he loved me and kissed me on the cheek. When I got back from the store an hour later, I found him dead. But there was something strange about his death. Apparently, just before Daddy died, he leaned over and rested his head on the chair beside the bed. What do you make of that?"

The minister wiped a tear from his eye and said, "I wish we could all go like that."

Who is sitting in your empty chair?

* *Assignment Whisper* *

June 15

Volunteer at a hospice today.

While it may be true that hospice care comes at the end of your life, there is still living to be done. Volunteering with hospice patients or in a hospice center does not mean what you might think.

Hospice specialists provide many services to improve the quality of life for patients. Assisting with medical needs, providing therapies, and supporting family members are just a few of the services provided by hospice care workers. Helping families navigate the maze of insurance rules frees families to spend time with their loved ones.

Some volunteer ideas include:

- ❖ Provide clerical support.
- ❖ Lead a Karaoke day.
- ❖ Sit with patients to give caregivers some time to themselves.
- ❖ Assist with grief counseling.
- ❖ Teach art classes or cooking classes.
- ❖ Decorate a hospice center.
- ❖ Plant flowers in the hospice center's garden.
- ❖ Assist with a fundraising.
- ❖ Note your ideas here.

For more information, visit www.hospicenet.org.

* Assignment Whisper *

June 16

In most cases, the birth of a baby is a joyous occasion. However, each year, almost 750,000 teenage women aged 15–19 become pregnant. The majority of these cases are not planned. Some are situations of rape or incest. Others are the result of peer pressure regarding sex.

Teen pregnancy also impacts the health of our young. In the United States, one in four sexually active teens become infected with a sexually transmitted disease every year. Teen pregnancy also impacts the dropout rate of our nation's next generation. Without a strong educational base, job opportunities will be limited for the rest of their lives.

A growing number of teens are taking vows of purity. The movement to preserve sexual relations until marriage is taking root in our nation. Weekend retreats and workshops can be found in most cities across the country.

Volunteer today to support this cause. Support the teens in your life to commit to purity. Visit this website for some ideas of ways you can help: www.generationsofvirtue.org, or look up Passport to Purity for materials to use at home.

* *Assignment Whisper* *

June 17

You say: "It's impossible"
God says: All things are possible (Luke 18:27)
You say: "I'm too tired"
God says: I will give you rest (Matthew 11:28-30)
You say: "Nobody really loves me"
God says: I love you (John 3:16 & John 13:34)
You say: "I can't go on"
God says: My grace is sufficient (II Corinthians 12:9 & Psalm91:15)
You say: "I can't figure things out"
God says: I will direct your steps(Proverbs 3:5-6)
You say: "I can't do it"
God says: You can do all things (Philippians 4:13)
You say: "I'm not able"
God says: I am able (II Corinthians 9:8)
You say: "It's not worth it"
God says: It will be worth it (Roman 8:28)
You say: "I can't forgive myself"
God says: I FORGIVE YOU (I John 1:9 & Romans 8:1)
You say: "I can't manage"
God says: I will supply all your needs(Philippians 4:19)
You say: "I'm afraid"
God says: I have not given you a spirit of fear (II Timothy 1:7)
You say: "I'm always worried and frustrated"
God says: Cast all your cares on ME (I Peter 5:7)
You say: "I don't have enough faith"
God says: I've given everyone a measure of faith (Romans 12:3)
You say: "I'm not smart enough"
God says: I give you wisdom (I Corinthians 1:30)
You say: "I feel all alone"
God says: I will never leave you or forsake you (Hebrews 13:5)

Author Unknown

* *Assignment Whisper* *

June 18

Then you will call upon me
and come and pray to me,
and I will listen to you.
You will seek me
and find me
when you seek me
with all your heart.

Jeremiah 29:12-13

Check your heart today. Is your heart seeking the Lord, or is your heart distracted by other things?

The Lord reminds us that when we pray, He will listen. Prayer is communication between you and God. However, it is not limited to words.

Is your "whispering" coming from your heart? Are you volunteering and serving others from a pure love of the Lord? Are you relying on Him to guide and sustain your efforts? Is your "whispering" a prayer in action to God?

Spend some time today listening to your heart and how you heart seeks the Lord. Remember, God is listening. What is your heart saying?

June 19

Babysit for a neighbor today.

The summer time fun might be turning the corner towards boredom in some houses. The vacation trip has yet to arrive, and school is still a long ways away. Those kids who were so excited about summer vacation are now wondering what to do with themselves.

Volunteer to babysit for a neighbor whose kids are getting restless today. If you have children, this will also entertain your brood. Variety always works to cure the monotony. Even if the kids are not the same ages or have the same interests, they will surely be able to stimulate each others' creative juices for one day.

By watching the children for a neighbor today, you will provide a break to the mother, too. Mothers are better able to inspire their kids through the remainder of the summer once they receive time to recharge their own batteries. This helps everyone to enjoy the time that they have together.

* *Assignment Whisper* *

June 20

Author and lecturer Leo Buscaglia once talked about a contest he was asked to judge. The purpose of the contest was to find the most caring child.

The winner was a four year old child whose next door neighbor was an elderly gentleman who had recently lost his wife. Upon seeing the man cry, the little boy went into the old gentleman's yard, climbed onto his lap, and just sat there. When his Mother asked what he had said to the neighbor, the little boy said, "Nothing, I just helped him cry"

Help someone cry today.

June 21

Therefore I tell you, whatever you ask for in prayer, believe that you have received it, and it will be yours.

Mark 11: 24

Have you ever heard the story about the farming community that was suffering from a long drought? Crops were close to failure for the third consecutive season. Finances were tight for everyone in town.

The community leaders decided to hold a prayer meeting for the much-needed rains. Everyone in town crowded into the local church to attend the prayer meeting.

Only one man brought an umbrella.

Do you pray as if you expect your prayers to be answered, or do you pray as if your words disappear in the wind?

Remember to carry an umbrella when you pray for rain.

June 22

Give your spouse a foot massage today.

Everyone loves a foot massage as well as a little special attention from their spouse. Spend a few minutes today paying special attention to your spouse by massaging his or her feet.

You do not need to be a professional masseuse to do this task. Special lotions or potions are not necessary. If you have them, that is nice, but not required. Do not let the lack of talent get in your way.

If possible, get the kids involved, too. Make it a family event. Let everyone enjoy pampering the family.

You may also want to include a Biblical history lesson here on the practice of washing feet. In John 13, Jesus washed the feet of his disciples. Create a family devotional while discovering Jesus' purpose and meaning in this activity.

* *Assignment Whisper* *

June 23

Dear Lord,

So far today, God, I've done all right. I haven't gossiped, haven't lost my temper, haven't been greedy, grumpy, nasty, selfish, or overindulgent. I'm really glad about that.

But in a few minutes, God, I'm going to get out of bed, and from then on, I'm probably going to need alot more help.

Thank you in Jesus' name.

AMEN!

Let no corrupt communication proceed out of your mouth, but what is good for necessary edification, that it may impart grace to the hearers.

Ephesians 4:29

June 24

Take a cookie to your dry cleaners today.

The dry cleaners are another one of those marginal jobs that most people take for granted. We may see these people on a regular basis, but do we even know their names? Do we take the time to see the person, or just look at them long enough to know that they gave us the correct clothes? A computer could not do their job, yet we sometimes treat these people as if they are automated.

Take the time today to chat with your dry cleaners. Let them know that you realize they are people, too.

Some fun ideas include:

❖Take them a cookie or a candy bar.
❖Bring your kids to sing silly songs.
❖Give them a card.
❖Take flowers from your garden.
❖Make some decorations for their lobby.
❖Smile at them and call them by name.
❖Note your ideas here.

* *Assignment Whisper* *

June 25

Donate hand sanitizers to the zoo gift shop or cafeteria.

Most zoos have petting areas. Your kids arrive at the gift shop or cafeteria after petting the animals. Imagine how much hand sanitizer your local zoo uses in a year. Think how many germs your kids would ingest if it were not provided.

The zoos also use hand sanitizers so that the kids do not transmit germs to the animals. Everyone says healthy when it is used.

Donate some hand sanitizer to the zoo. If you are not able to do this, write a letter to the zoo thanking them for providing this to the patrons. Set a jar on your counter for loose change to begin a fund to raise money to donate sanitizer.

June 26

Just Checking In
Author Unknown

A minister passing through his church
in the middle of the day,
Decided to pause by the altar
and see who had come to pray.

Just then the back door opened,
a man came down the aisle,
The minister frowned as he saw
the man hadn't shaved in a while.

His shirt was kinda shabby
and his coat was worn and frayed,
the man knelt, he bowed his head,
Then rose and walked away.

In the days that followed,
each noon time came this chap,
each time he knelt just for a moment,
A lunch pail in his lap.

Well, the minister's suspicions grew,
with robbery a main fear,
He decided to stop the man and ask him,
"What are you doing here?"

The old man said, he worked down the road.
Lunch was half an hour.
Lunchtime was his prayer time,
For finding strength and power.

* *Assignment Whisper* *

"I stay only moments, see,
because the factory is so far away;
as I kneel here talking to the Lord,
This is kinda what I say:

"I just came again to tell you, Lord.
How happy I've been,
Since we found each other's friendship
And you took away my sin.

Don't know much of how to pray,
But I think about you every day.
So, Jesus, this is Jim
Checking in today."

The minister feeling foolish,
told Jim that was fine.
He told the man he was welcome
To come and pray just anytime.

Time to go, Jim smiled, said "Thanks."
He hurried to the door.
The minister knelt at the altar,
he'd never done it before.

His cold heart melted, warmed with love,
and met with Jesus there.
As the tears flowed, in his heart,
he repeated old Jim's prayer:

"I just came again to tell you, Lord.
How happy I've been,
Since we found each other's friendship
And you took away my sin.

* *Assignment Whisper* *

Don't know much of how to pray,
But I think about you every day.
So, Jesus, this is me
Checking in today."

Past noon one day, the minister noticed
that old Jim hadn't come.
As more days passed without Jim,
he began to worry some.

At the factory, he asked about him,
learning he was ill.
The hospital staff was worried,
But he'd given them a thrill.

The week that Jim was with them,
Brought changes in the ward.
His smiles, a joy contagious.
Changed people, were his reward.

The head nurse couldn't understand
why Jim was so glad,
when no flowers, calls or cards came,
Not a visitor he had.

The minister stayed by his bed,
He voiced the nurse's concern:
No friends came to show they cared.
He had nowhere to turn.

Looking surprised, old Jim spoke up
and with a winsome smile;
"the nurse is wrong, she couldn't know,
that in here all the while everyday at noon

* *Assignment Whisper* *

He's here, a dear friend of mine, you see,
He sits right down, takes my hand,
Leans over and says to me:

"I just came again to tell you, Jim
How happy I have been,
Since we found this friendship,
And I took away your sin.

Always love to hear you pray,
I think about you each day,
And so Jim, this is Jesus
Checking in today."

* *Assignment Whisper* *

June 27

Since it is summer and everyone enjoys a good summer book, I would like to recommend that you read the Bible. Yes, read the entire Bible - cover to cover.

Most of us have read parts of it. Some of us have read all of it. Many have thought seriously about reading it someday. Well, today is the day.

If you have never read the entire Bible before, let me warn you that some parts of it are rather dry reading. However, I encourage you to endure these parts and not miss a single word. God put them there for a reason. Each and every part of the Bible was included for our own good and edification.

Some books of the Bible will move your heart and soul. There will be times when you wonder how you missed the truths contained in the pages. Cherish these passages and know that there are more to come. Each time you read the Bible, God will illuminate more and more for you. Ask God for wisdom as you read.

But the wisdom that comes from heaven is first of all pure; then peace-loving, considerate, submissive, full of mercy and good fruit, impartial and sincere.

James 3:17

June 28

Crabby Old Woman
Author Unknown

What do you see, nurses? What do you see?
What are you thinking, when you're looking at me?
A crabby old woman, not very wise, Uncertain of
habit, with faraway eye.

Who dribbles her food, and makes no reply, When
you say in a loud voice, "I do wish you'd try!"
Who seems not to notice, the things that you do,
And forever is losing, a stocking or shoe?

Who, resisting or not, lets you do as you will, With
bathing and feeding, the long day to fill?
Is that what you're thinking? Is that what you see?
Then open your eyes, nurse, you're not looking at
me.

I'll tell you who I am, as I sit here so still, As I do at
your bidding, as I eat at your will.
I'm a small child of ten, with a father and mother,
Brothers and sisters, who love one another.

A young girl of sixteen, with wings on her feet,
Dreaming that soon now, a lover she'll meet.
A bride soon at twenty, my heart gives a leap,
Remembering the vows, that I promised to keep.

At twenty-five now, I have young of my own, Who
need me to guide, and a secure happy home.
A woman of thirty, my young now grown fast, Bound
to each other, with ties that should last.

* *Assignment Whisper* *

At forty, my young sons, have grown and are gone,
But my man's beside me, to see I don't mourn.
At fifty once more, babies play round my knee,
Again we know children, my loved one and me.

Dark days are upon me, my husband is dead, I look
at the future, I shudder with dread.
For my young are all rearing, young of their own,
And I think of the years, and the love that I've
known.

I'm now an old woman, and nature is cruel, 'Tis jest
to make old age, look like a fool.
The body, it crumbles, grace and vigor depart, There
is now a stone, where I once had a heart.

But inside this old carcass, a young girl still dwells,
And now and again, my battered heart swells.
I remember the joys, I remember the pain, And I'm
loving and living, life over again.

I think of the years, all too few, gone too fast, And
accept the stark fact, that nothing can last.
So open your eyes, people, open and see, Not a
crabby old woman; look closer... see ME!!

* *Assignment Whisper* *

June 29

Do something for a volunteer fireman today.

If your area does not have volunteer fireman, honor those fire fighters who are paid to put out flames. You might also whisper to someone who works at the fire academy or police academy.

The duties performed by the fire fighters go far beyond extinguishing fires. They also save lives, risk their lives for your pets, attempt to salvage your personal belongings, provide first aide services, and teach safety classes to anyone who asks. These brave people train their bodies and minds to be prepared to put themselves in dangerous situations. They sacrifice time with their own families in order to save your family if the need arises. They often need to purchase their own supplies when budgets are tight.

Here are some ideas to brighten their day:

❖ Take cookies.
❖ Write a thank you note. Deliver it in person or put it in the mail.
❖ Cut a bouquet of fresh flowers from your garden.
❖ Sing cheerful songs with your children.
❖ Donate non-perishables to their pantry.
❖ Order pizza delivered for lunch.
❖ Donate stuffed animals for them to give to children who are victims of fire or accidents.
❖ Note your ideas here.

June 30

Emergency Phone Numbers
Author Unknown

When in sorrow, call John 14.
When men fail you, call Psalm 27.
If you want to be fruitful, call John 15.
When you have sinned, call Psalm 51.
When you worry, call Matthew 6:19-34.
When you are in danger, call Psalm 91.
When God seems far away, call Psalm 139.
When your faith needs stirring, call Hebrews 11.
When you are lonely and fearful, call Psalm 23.
When you grow bitter and critical, call 1 Cor. 13.
For Paul's secret to happiness, call Col. 3:12-17.
For idea of Christianity, call 1 Cor. 5:15-19.
When you feel down and out, call Romans 8:31-
When you want peace and rest, call Matt. 11:25-30.
When the world seems bigger than God, call Psalm 90.
When you want Christian assurance, call Romans 8:1-
30.
When you leave home for labor or travel, call Psalm 121.
When your prayers grow narrow or selfish, call Psalm 67.
For a great invention/opportunity, call Isaiah 55.
When you want courage for a task, call Joshua 1.
How to get along with fellow men, call Romans 12.
When you think of investments/returns, call Mark 10.
If you are depressed, call Psalm 27.
If your pocketbook is empty, call Psalm 37.
If you're losing confidence in people, call 1 Cor. 13.
If people seem unkind, call John 15.
If discouraged about your work, call Psalm 126.
If you find the world growing small and yourself great,
call Psalm 19.

July 1

From the beginning of time, land has been an issue. Adam and Eve were the first humans on earth as well as the first people to be removed from their land. (See Genesis 3:23-24.)

Every nation since Adam struggles to hold onto their land. Battles have been fought in every generation for real estate.

Our nation today is comprised of a greater number of nationalities than at any other point in history. Americans are continually expanding the cultural influences that shape our nation. Every four years a new president is confronted with unique situations from the increasing demand for cultural sensitivities.

None of this is a surprise to God. Since His creation of Eden, He has had a plan for His nation. From Genesis to Revelation, His plan is revealed, and that plan encompasses every nation.

Begin in Acts 10:34, which states:

Then Peter began to speak: "I now realize how true it is that God does not show favoritism but accepts men from every nation who fear him and do what is right. You know the message God sent to the people of Israel, telling the good news of peace through Jesus Christ, who is Lord of all.

As you whisper to others during this month when we celebrate our nation's birth, remember that we all belong to God's nation as well. Consider your countrymen from that point of view.

* *Assignment Whisper* *

July 2

Just as God has a plan for His nation, families must also have a plan.

Talk to your spouse today about your family's future. Discuss your immediate goals as well as far reaching goals. Develop a plan together to achieve these goals for your family. Encompass all types of goals:

❖Financial goals
❖Career goals
❖Family planning goals
❖Emotional goals
❖Spiritual goals
❖Entertainment/vacation goals
❖Educational goals
❖Health goals
❖Household trash removal goals (Sorry. I just could not resist adding this one!)

Remind your spouse that you are happy with your life together. Your goals for the future will build on what you have accomplished this far. Talk about how much you have enjoyed your life together to this point and how excited you are about your future together.

The goal of the day is planning for the future. This is not about placing blame for goals not yet achieved. Spend the day sharing your excitement about moving forward.

* *Assignment Whisper* *

July 3

Now that you and your spouse have a plan for your family, spend today helping your kids develop a plan for their own future.

Depending on the age of your child, this task may be silly or heart-wrenching. If your five year old's plan is focused on how he will eat once his baby teeth start falling out, flow with it. Every age has its own set of concerns, and all are valid.

If your teenager is mapping their college degree plan, start another pot of coffee. Remember how you felt when you did the same thing. Degree plans might not feel all that important once you have graduated, but to those in college or just entering college, degree plans can be overwhelming.

If your children are not at an age or stage of life where goals for the future seem important, ask them to make some goals anyway. Spend some time encouraging the idea even when the details are fuzzy. Success is easier to obtain when the finish line is well-defined. Some day your children will remember how you encouraged the idea and make plans of their own.

Once your children have shared their goals with you, ask them how you can contribute to their success. Add your contribution to their goals to your plans for your future. Show your children that you are all in this together even when the goals are individual.

* *Assignment Whisper* *

July 4

Today, on the anniversary of the birth of our nation, do something for a soldier.

Whether our nation is currently at war or not, the freedoms that we enjoy come at a price. Every life sacrificed in the line of duty was given to protect our liberties and way of life. Today is the day to honor those who have served.

Some ideas include:

❖ Write a letter or send a care package to a soldier.
  o www.anysoldier.com
  o www.letssaythankyou.com
  o www.asoldierswishlist.org
❖ Volunteer to teach a class at a military base.
❖ Place a wreath on a soldier's grave at a veteran's cemetery.
❖ Pray for our troops.
❖ Invite a military wife to lunch.
❖ Donate to Operation Purple.
❖ Visit Fisher House.
❖ Distribute flags to your city's parade.
❖ Note your ideas here.

* *Assignment Whisper* *

July 5

Today pray specifically for the President and his family.

You may not have voted for him, but he is still the President. You may not agree with his politics, his voting record, his morals, or his religion. Put that aside for one day, and pray for him as the nation recovers from yesterday's festivities.

Remember to pray for the President's wife as well. Being the First Lady is a difficult task. There is no job assignment or specific instructions that outline her duties. She cannot resign. She cannot speak her mind. She represents our country with style and grace that go beyond what most woman naturally possess. She also will learn to tune out more criticism than any other woman in town.

Include the President's family in your prayers as well today. They, like the First Lady, are part of the package and yet separate at the same time. The President's children and extended family members are all scrutinized and threatened. Yet they must hold their opinions and smile through it all.

Regardless of his politics, the President is a person, too. Lift him and his family up in prayer today as our nation continues through its growing pains.

* *Assignment Whisper* *

July 6

In the New Testament, "freedom" in Christ is defined as:
1) release from bondage or imprisonment
2) forgiveness or pardon, of sins (letting them go as if they had never been committed), remission of the penalty

Webster defines "freedom" as:
1. the absence of necessity, coercion, or constraint in choice or action
2. liberation from slavery or restraint or from the power of another : independence
3. the quality or state of being exempt or released usually from something onerous

After reflecting on the freedoms of our nation, today is time to reflect on the things that are holding you personally in bondage. Are there polluted memories, past hurts, annoying habits, or unhealthy thoughts that are preventing you from realizing your full potential?

In Christ, we have no need for these things any longer. We have forgiveness of sins and freedom from the damage sin has done in our lives. Claim your victory over sin today, in Jesus' name.

Therefore, if anyone is in Christ, he is a new creation; the old has gone, the new has come!
2 Corinthians 5:17

* *Assignment Whisper* *

July 7

A Soldier's Cards
This story derived from a song
by Tex Ritter & T. Texas Tyler.

It was quiet that day, the guns and the mortars, and land mines for some reason hadn't been heard. The young soldier knew it was Sunday, the holiest day of the week. As he was sitting there, he got out an old deck of cards and laid them out across his bunk.

Just then an army sergeant came in and said, "Why aren't you with the rest of the platoon?"

The soldier replied, "I thought I would stay behind and spend some time with the Lord."

The sergeant said, "Looks to me like you're going to play cards."

The soldier said, "No, sir. You see, since we are not allowed to have Bibles or other spiritual books in this country, I've decided to talk to the Lord by studying this deck of cards."

The sergeant asked in disbelief, "How will you do that?"

"You see the Ace, Sergeant? It reminds me that there is only one God.

The Two represents the two parts of the Bible, Old and New Testaments.

The Three represents the Father, Son, and the Holy Ghost.

The Four stands for the Four Gospels: Matthew, Mark, Luke and John.

The Five is for the five virgins that were ten but only five of them were glorified.

The Six is for the six days it took God to create the Heavens and Earth. The Seven is for the day God rested after making His Creation.

* Assignment Whisper *

The Eight is for the family of Noah and his wife, their three sons and their wives - the eight people God spared from the flood that destroyed the earth.

The Nine is for the lepers that Jesus cleansed of leprosy. He cleansed ten, but nine never thanked Him.

The Ten represents the Ten Commandments that God handed down to Moses on tablets made of stone.

The Jack is a reminder of Satan, one of God's first angels, but he got kicked out of heaven for his sly and wicked ways and is now the joker of eternal hell.

The Queen stands for the Virgin Mary.

The King stands for Jesus, for He is the King of all kings.

When I count the dots on all the cards, I come up with 365 total, one for every day of the year.

There are a total of 52 cards in a deck; each is a week - 52 weeks in a year. The four suits represent the four seasons: Spring, Summer, Fall and Winter. Each suit has thirteen cards - there are exactly thirteen weeks in a quarter.

So when I want to talk to God and thank Him, I just pull out this old deck of cards and they remind me of all that I have to be thankful for."

The sergeant just stood there. After a minute, with tears in his eyes and pain in his heart, he said, "Soldier, can I borrow that deck of cards?"

Please let this be a reminder and take time to pray for all of our soldiers who are being sent away, putting their lives on the line fighting for us.

Prayer for the Military. Please keep the wheel rolling. It will only take a few seconds of your time, but it'll be worth it to read on....

* *Assignment Whisper* *

Lord, hold our troops in your loving hands. Protect them as they protect us. Bless them and their families for the selfless acts they perform for us in our time of need. I ask this in the name of Jesus, our Lord and Savior.

July 8

Pray for your state's senators today. Write them a letter to thank them for their service to our nation.

Even if you do not agree with their politics or their voting record, they are still people. Encourage them to persevere. Remind them that the nation supports them.

Each state has two senators. You can locate the names of your state's senators at this website: www.senate.gov/general/contact_information/senators_cfm.cfm.

Senators are elected by the people of their state to serve a six year term. There is no limit to the number of terms that a senator can serve.

Remember the senator's family as well today.

July 9

Pray for the mayor of your city today.

If you live in a small town, you may know your mayor personally. If you live in a large city, you might not know the name of your mayor. Either way, many people are not aware of their mayor's agenda or accomplishments.

Spend some time today learning the achievements of your current major. Investigate what his goals are for the future of your city. Think about ways that you can contribute to these goals.

Pay a visit to your mayor's office today. Tell them thank you for their service. Ask them for information about events and activities in your city.

If you have children, take your children with you. Arrange for a tour of city hall. Teach your children the duties of the mayor's office and the jobs performed by his staff. Discuss the differences between local, state, and federal governments with your kids. Teach them how the wheels of government turn.

July 10

Today is a continuation of yesterday's whisper. While you were in the mayor's office yesterday, you probably met his secretary and support staff. Pray for these people today.

It is common in government, business, churches, and organizations that the secretary and staff are the people who ensures that things get done. They are the backbone of the public person who is in charge, yet the staff rarely receive acknowledgement for their contributions.

Recognize the mayor's silent support staff today. Now that you have met them, write them thank you notes. Tell your friends and neighbors about these people. Sing their praises even if you do not agree with their politics.

If your children were with you yesterday in the mayor's office, have your children write thank you notes as well. They could draw a picture or record a greeting of thanks on a tape recorder.

* *Assignment Whisper* *

July 11

Donate your old cell phones to Cell Phones for Soldiers today.

Dig through your drawers for those phones that you never use. Ask your kids to donate the cell phones that they play with as toys. Donate them to the group that turns them into phone cards for soldiers.

Cell Phones for Soldiers' mission is to help our troops call home. Donated cell phones are converted to cash. The cash is then used to purchase prepaid calling cards for American troops. Since 2004, this group has been helping military families stay connected even though they are miles apart. The organization was started by teens siblings Brittany and Robbie Bergquist.

For more information, visit their website at:
www.cellphonesforsoldiers.com.

The website contains information on drop off centers across the nation. Cell phones can also be mailed to the following address:

Cell Phone Recycling Center
2555 Bishop Circle West
Dexter, Michigan 48130-9916

Turn your trash into the treasure of a phone call for a soldier. It does not get any easier than this.

* *Assignment Whisper* *

July 12

Pray for your state representatives today. Write them a letter to thank them for their service to our nation. Even if you do not agree with their politics or their voting record, they are still people. Encourage them to persevere. Remind them that the nation supports them.

Each state receives representation in the House in proportion to its population but is entitled to at least one representative. Representatives serve two year terms. There are no term limits.

You can locate the names of your state's representatives at this website: www.house.gov/house/Memberwww_by_State.shtml

For mailing addresses to the representative from your area, visit this website: writerep.house.gov/writerep/welcome.shtml.

Research the duties and responsibilities of the House of Representatives so that you can teach it to your children.

Remember the representative's family as well today.

* *Assignment Whisper* *

July 13

...What does the Lord require of you? To act justly and to love mercy and to walk humbly with your God.

Micah 6:8

These words found in the book of Micah apply to all nations and all people. They do not tell us to act justly just to those people we like and respect. It does not encourage us to love mercy only when it is comfortable to do. It does not invite us to walk humbly with God only when we see God walking with our friends.

Consider what the character of our planet would look like if we applied these words to all nations and all peoples. What if nations were able to act justly to all nations? How would the love of mercy on a global scale manifest itself? What if people from every nation and culture were able to walk together with God in pure humility and love at the same time? Reflect on what the world would look like to the future generations if we all practiced this idea today.

What can you do today to a make this happen?

* *Assignment Whisper* *

July 14

Pray for your local judges today.

Perhaps you have met a local judge in a traffic court or worse. Maybe you have had unpleasant experiences with those in the court system where you live. Regardless of the circumstances, pray for the judges today.

Teach your children about the duties and responsibilities of the local courts and judges. Arrange for a tour of the courts so that they can experience an average day for a judge.

Here are some ideas to brighten their day:
- ❖ Take cookies.
- ❖ Write a thank you note. Deliver it in person or put it in the mail.
- ❖ Cut a bouquet of fresh flowers from your garden.
- ❖ Bring your children to sing cheerful songs.
- ❖ Donate air fresheners.
- ❖ Supply hand lotion.
- ❖ Order pizza delivered for lunch.
- ❖ Note your ideas here.

July 15

Send a card to a military personnel today.

Visit www.LetsSayThanks.com to send a free card to a soldier.

This website allows you to send a free card to a member of the armed services from the privacy of your own home. Simply select a design from their gallery of pictures contributed by children. Then select one of their prepared sentiments for your card or compose a note of your own. After hitting the send button, Xerox prints your card and delivers it to a deployed soldier.

This website also includes notes of thanks from the soldiers who have received these cards. It is overwhelming to read their thanks for something as simple as a card from a stranger.

If you or someone in your family is an artist, consider designing a card to submit to the site.

Bookmark this page today and visit it daily. Send a card and brighten someone's day. It only takes a minute but will mean the world to a deployed soldier.

July 16

Pray for the governor of your state today.

Spend some time today learning the achievements of your current governor. Investigate what his goals are for the future of your state. Think about ways in which you can contribute to these goals.

Pay a visit to your governor's office if possible. Tell them thank you for their service. Ask them for information about events and activities in your state.

If you have children, take your children with you. Arrange for a tour of the capital. Teach your children the duties of the governor's office and the jobs performed by his staff. Discuss the differences between local, state, and federal governments with your kids. Teach them how the wheels of government turn.

Visit this website for contact information: www.usa.gov/Contact/Governors.shtml.

Remember to pray for your governor's family today as well.

* *Assignment Whisper* *

July 17

Read the Constitution of the United States today.

Most of us read this in school years ago. However, can you honestly say that you remember what it says? Read the entire Constitution today.

Last year while visiting Washington DC, I had the opportunity to visit the Senate Chamber. I was fascinated and awed by the building as well as the process. The ushers were very personable and encouraged questions. While talking with the usher about the duties of the Senate, she handed me a pocket-sized booklet that contained the text of the Constitution. She said that one of the senators printed them so that all the senators could carry them in their suit coat pockets every day.

These senators are elected by you and me. They represent our interests in the government. We elect them to protect the Constitution. Before voting, I encourage you to know the document that you are entrusting to these people.

The entire Constitution can be found at: www.usconstitution.net/const.html. And, yes, it can be digested in one sitting.

Make notes about what you learned.

July 18

After reading the Constitution yesterday, today memorize the Preamble to the Constitution. It is very short and easy to remember.

We the People of the United States, in Order to form a more perfect Union, establish Justice, insure domestic Tranquility, provide for the common defense, promote the general Welfare, and secure the Blessings of Liberty to ourselves and our Posterity, do ordain and establish this Constitution for the United States of America.

Be on familiar terms with your nation's government. Commit these things to memory and teach them to your children. How can the foundation of our nation be preserved in future generations if we do not teach it to our children?

July 19

An eye witness account from New York City, on a cold day in December, some years ago: A little boy, about 10-years-old, was standing before a shoe store on the roadway, barefooted, peering through the window, and shivering with cold.

A lady approached the young boy and said, "My, but you're in such deep thought staring in that window!"

"I was asking God to give me a pair of shoes," was the boy's reply.

The lady took him by the hand, went into the store, and asked the clerk to get half a dozen pairs of socks for the boy. She then asked if he could give her a basin of water and a towel. He quickly brought them to her.

She took the little fellow to the back part of the store and, removing her gloves, knelt down, washed his little feet, and dried them with the towel. By this time, the clerk had returned with the socks. Placing a pair upon the boy's feet, she purchased him a pair of shoes.

She tied up the remaining pairs of socks and gave them to him. She patted him on the head and said, "No doubt, you will be more comfortable now."

As she turned to go, the astonished kid caught her by the hand, and looking up into her face, with tears in his eyes, asked her, "Are you God's wife?"

Are foreigners who we perceive them to be?

July 20

Thank your local 911 dispatcher today.

I am fortunate that our family has never experienced an emergency that required a call to 911. However, I am thankful that these people are on the job. I cannot imagine needing a fire truck, dialing 911, and listening to a recording.

The dispatchers at the 911 center are trained in a variety of duties. Not only do they answer the phone, they are the calm in the middle of personal crisis. They evaluate each situation and determine the proper course of action.

Dispatchers also take their share of abuse. Not all calls to 911 are appropriate. Some callers are verbally abusive. Some calls are pranks. Others cause nightmares that no one wants to discuss. Through it all, the dispatcher is there to assist the next caller.

Here are some ideas to brighten their day:

- ❖ Take cookies.
- ❖ Write a thank you note. Deliver it in person or put it in the mail.
- ❖ Cut a bouquet of fresh flowers from your garden.
- ❖ Bring your children to sing cheerful songs.
- ❖ Draw a funny picture to cheer up their desk.
- ❖ Order pizza delivered for lunch.
- ❖ Note your ideas here.

* *Assignment Whisper* *

July 21

Today pray specifically for the Vice President and his family.

You may not have voted for him, but he is still the Vice President. You may not agree with his politics, his voting record, his morals, or his religion. Yet he is still the Vice President.

Remember to pray for the Vice President's wife as well. She has no job assignment or specific instructions that outline her duties. She cannot resign. She cannot speak her mind. She represents our country with style and grace that go beyond what most woman naturally possess. She also will learn to tune out more criticism than any other woman in town while being compared to the First Lady.

Include the Vice President's family in your prayers as well today. They are part of the package and yet separate at the same time. The Vice President's children and extended family members are all scrutinized and threatened. Yet they must hold their opinions and smile through it all.

Regardless of his politics, the Vice President is a person, too. Lift him and his family up in prayer today.

* *Assignment Whisper* *

July 22

Volunteer at Fisher House today.

If you live near a veteran's hospital, you have probably heard of Fisher House. Their website states:

"Because members of the military and their families are stationed worldwide and must often travel great distances for specialized medical care, Fisher House™ Foundation donates "comfort homes," built on the grounds of major military and VA medical centers. These homes enable family members to be close to a loved one at the most stressful times - during the hospitalization for an unexpected illness, disease, or injury."

Fisher House is similar to a hotel for families of patients in a VA hospital. It is an oasis of hope and support for those who are helping a veteran through their recovery.

Volunteer opportunities at Fisher House vary from location to location. Interior decorators could facilitate decorating a new home. Fundraising and community awareness are essential to their ability to provide services to families. If you enjoy cooking, deliver a home cooked meal to those families who are far from their own homes.

Visit www.fisherhouse.org for more information.

July 23

Read a book about American history. Learn about the nation's founding fathers, or relive the struggles to independence through a movie.

Our nation is not where we are by default. Many people and circumstances shaped what America has become. Spend some time this summer learning the history of the nation. You might be surprised how fascinating it can be.

For movie suggestions, visit www.teachwithmovies.org/us-history-culture-subject-list.htm.

For book suggestions, any librarian or bookstore employee can assist you in making a good selection. There are numerous biographies of presidents worth reading. The amount of information documented about the Mayflower, its passengers, and its voyage is astounding.

Whether you choose a book or a movie, once you get hooked on American history, you will want to learn as much as you can. Get your kids excited about history, too. Make a monthly date to spend the evening as a family learning about history.

* *Assignment Whisper* *

July 24

Do something for the staff at a veteran's hospital today.

Volunteers often target patients, which is a wonderful thing. However, do not forget the staff. It takes a special person to work in the medical field. Now add to that medical skill the knowledge that every patient is there as a result of their service to their country. Include the bureaucratic red tape of working in a government facility. Add all of that together, and you get a very special staff person.

This website will help you locate a VA hospital in your area: www1.va.gov/directory.

July 25

Volunteer for a political campaign or candidate.

You may decide to do something locally or nationally. You might want to assist behind the scenes or at the head of the crowd. Whatever your interest, select a politician or a political cause that moves you and lend your support.

Most people that I know, myself included, have definite opinions about politicians and how they are handling current events. The media is quick to tell us about the corruption on the campaign trails during election seasons. Find out for yourself what it is like. Discover firsthand how elections are won or lost.

If you have ever wondered how elections would have turned out if everyone had voted or become involved in the candidates they supported, this is your chance. Step up to the plate and get involved.

July 26

Place flowers on the grave of a veteran today.

You do not necessarily need to know the veteran. If you do not live close to a veteran's cemetery, you are sure to find veterans buried in your local cemetery. You may want to contact the cemetery caretaker as they may know of a grave that is not visited often.

You could also plan now to donate to the Wreaths Across America. Their website is: www.wreaths-across-america.org.

Perhaps you could start a fundraiser now to promote this cause later in the year. Maybe you could encourage others in your community to start their own wreath laying ceremony this year.

Military families relocate often during their time of service. It is not always practical for family members to visit the graves of their loved ones at specific times of the year. Stand in for the family of a military family today and honor their service by decorating a grave.

* *Assignment Whisper* *

July 27

<u>Volunteering fact</u>
According to www.nationalmuseum.af.mil:
"Volunteers contributed 92,217 hours of time in 2007 to the Museum of United States Air Force.... This is worth $1,800,134 and 44 person-years of productivity. "

Investigate military museums close to your home. Find out what volunteer opportunities exist for you and your family. Consider how you can contribute to the preservation of our nation's history by volunteering at military museums.

This is a wonderful website to begin your search: www.olive-drab.com/od_history_museums_us.php.

Another helpful resource is: www.militarymuseum.org/armylinks.html.

July 28

Thank that staff at the local military recruiting office today.

If you have sons or daughters who are considering a career in the military, this may be an uncomfortable thought for you. However, the staff in the recruiting offices serve a valuable service to our nation. While we are fortunate that our nation does not currently enforce the draft, their job still needs to be performed.

Select a branch of the service: Army, Navy, Marines, Air Force, National Guard. Find the nearest recruiting office to your home. The website www.military.com might be helpful in this hunt.

* *Assignment Whisper* *

July 29

Volunteer at a national park today.

If you do not live close to a national park, write a letter to the staff at a national park to thank them for their service. Let them know how much you appreciate their dedication to preserving our nation and its parks.

Visit www.nps.gov for more information on the parks in our nation. You might be surprised at what you find on the list. If your family is able to take a vacation yet this summer, consider visiting one of the parks.

If you cannot visit in person, contact your local library for videos about various parks. The website www.nps.gov contains materials to make a curriculum about each park as well as distance learning options. Your family could take a virtual vacation to any park of your choosing. Have your kids develop a travel plan for a future visit to a park.

July 30

Read historical markers in your area today.

We have all driven past them, considered stopping from time to time. They are an amazing number of historical markers across the nation. Each of them tell a unique story, and these stories are worth documenting.

Visit www.hmdb.org to find the markers nearest to you.

If you do not find any near your home, visit them online and learn more about them.

Create some fun in your family by having your children place their own historical markers. Poster board, a stick, and some creativity are all that are needed to record significant events in your own lives. You might be astonished at the events and places that your children want to memorialize. Take photographs of their sites and create a scrapbook if the locations are not practical to permanently leave your signs.

July 31

Think of your vision for this nation. Where do you
want to see the nation in ten years, twenty years,
fifty years? What do you want this country to look
like for your grandchildren and their grandchildren?
What legacy do you want your generation to leave to
the next? What do you wish your ancestors had
done differently to shape the world as you know it
today?

Consider the ways that you can help to make that
vision come true. What can you do today so that
your vision becomes a reality for your descendents?
What can you contribute on a local and national
level? What can you teach your children today that
they can pass along to future generations?

Do not take this task lightly. Our future depends
on it.

* *Assignment Whisper* *

August 1

Today's whispering assignment focuses on forgiveness.

God's definition of forgiveness centers around freedom. In the Old Testament, the word forgiveness is translated as a pardon, purging, or reconciliation between people or between people and God. God pardons our sins and purges their effect from our lives. Therefore, we can be reconciled to God due to the elimination of sin.

The New Testament authors define forgiveness as liberty, deliverance, or to be let alone. Again, we see the separating effects of sin. Eliminating the impact of our transgressions restores fellowship with God.

Spend some time today contemplating the reoccurring sins in your life. Do not let yourself categorize them into small, large, significant, or menial. Sin is sin. Take your sins to God and ask for His forgiveness with a pure heart.

Bear with each other and forgive whatever grievances you may have against one another. Forgive as the Lord forgave you.

Colossians 3:13

* *Assignment Whisper* *

August 2

You want me to do what? Yes, I want you to forgive your spouse today.

Even if you have the most wonderful partner in the world, chances are high that you can think of one thing that you need to forgive him or her for doing or saying. If that thing comes to mind quickly, forgive your spouse for it now. If that thing does not immediately pop into your head, do not dwell on it. Be thankful that you have nothing between the two of you.

If your spouse is not your definition of an ideal life partner, forgive him or her for the dominant character flaws. Perhaps you believed the person would reform after you exchanged vows. Maybe you felt that your love would help him or her overcome things in the past. Forgive your spouse for all of those things.

While verbal apologies are valuable, it is most important that forgiveness comes from your heart. Forgiveness from the mouth is temporary and fleeting. Forgiveness from the heart is a life changing event for both of you. Make today's reconciliation originate from the depth of your soul.

* *Assignment Whisper* *

August 3

Today's whisper is an extension of yesterday's idea. Forgive your children today.

If you have more than one child, forgive each one for something unique to his or her personality. Remind them that you love them no matter what their life choices may be. Help them to know that you are happy to be their parent despite the little things they do that bother you.

The things that you say will depend on the child's age. Be sure to take into account your child's emotional age as well as chronological age. Some kids can handle more information than others. Choose your words carefully before speaking to your child today. Ensure that what you say and how you say it will build your child up and not scar your relationship.

If you do not have children, perhaps you have a niece or nephew that needs today's whisper from you. Consider what children in your family could light up from hearing words of reconciliation from you.

If you do not have children but plan to have them in the future, spend some time today thinking about having a forgiving heart toward your future children. They are bound to need your forgiveness at some point in their lives. Prepare yourself for that day now.

* *Assignment Whisper* *

August 4

Forgive a relative that you do not really like.

We all have family members that are somehow different. How many of us left family reunions pondering whether or not we were adopted? Siblings raised in the same house by the same parents turn out to be completely different individuals. Aunts, uncles, cousins, and in-laws can baffle the most forgiving person in the room.

Think of the relative that makes you shake your head in disbelief. What is it about this person that really bothers you? Whatever it is, forgive this person today. They are who they are regardless of how you feel about them. Accept them for the person they are.

What follows may be a wonderful relationship or perhaps just a quiet truce. Whatever the immediate result, let the forgiveness enter your heart today. Let the relationship grow from your commitment to forgiveness. One day you both may look back on this day and laugh together.

August 5

National Night Out should be sometime this week. Visit www.nationalnightout.org for more information about events in your area.

If it is not too late, organize an event or gathering for your neighborhood. Recruit the neighbors you have met this year through your whispering. Gather those you know to meet those you who are still strangers.

If you do not live in an area that is safe to walk at night, spend the evening at a friend or relative's house. It is always a good idea to know the people who live close to your loved ones.

Involve your entire family and encourage your neighbors to do the same. Kids need friends as much as adults do. It is important for your children to know what kids are supposed to be in the neighborhood and who might be there for ill pursuits.

When you visit the National Night Out website, take a few moments to read about Project 365 as well. If you are not able to participate this year, you will find some ideas to help prepare for next year.

* *Assignment Whisper* *

August 6

Help a high school student fill out college paperwork today.

With the beginning of the semester just weeks away, help a college student start the school year on the right foot. Sorting through the paperwork required to register and secure housing can be a daunting task. Your assistance and support might make all the difference to someone new to the chore.

Remember what it was like to be entering college for the first time. Remember the excitement of meeting new people. Recall the anticipation of meeting your teachers and hearing the workload for the semester. Feel the anxiety of learning your way around campus. Does that bring back memories?

If you know any first time college students who are preparing to start classes this fall, help them in any way that you can. Volunteer to walk the campus with them to learn their way around. Coach them on the importance of surrounding themselves with the right people. Encourage them to ask for help when they need it. Instill confidence in them as they enter this new phase of their lives.

* *Assignment Whisper* *

August 7

A boy asks his father to explain the differences among irritation, aggravation, and frustration.

His father picks up the phone and dials a number at random. When the phone is answered, he asks, "Can I speak to Alf, please?"

"No! There's no one called Alf here," says the person who answered the phone.

His father hangs up. "That's irritation," he says.

He picks up the phone again, dials the same number, and asks for Alf a second time.

"No. There's no one here called Alf. Go away. If you call again I shall phone the police," the person says.

His father hangs up the phone and says, "That's aggravation."

"Then what's frustration?" asks his son.

The father picks up the phone and dials the same number a third time.

"Hello, this is Alf. Have I received any calls?" he asks casually.

Who did you irritate today?

Who did you aggravate today?

Who did you frustrate today?

Sincerely ask forgiveness for your behavior from everyone targeted by your disrespect.

August 8

Forgive yourself today.

Whatever has been nagging at your conscience, forgive yourself for it. Perhaps it is something you said to someone. Maybe it is something you did that has left you with a guilty conscience. It might be something that you did *not* do or are currently refusing to do that has you bothered. Whatever it is, forgive yourself for it today.

If the thing that nags at your conscious is something that involves another person, consider apologizing face to face. It is not always possible or advisable to have these discussions, however, depending on the situation. You might try writing a letter expressing your regret even if you decide not to mail it. Writing a poem or a song about the situation may be more appealing to you.

Carrying around old baggage of unforgiven sins is not something that benefits anyone. Jesus' redemptive act on the cross freed us from the need to be burdened by sins ever again. Forgive yourself as Jesus already forgave you. Put down the cross. Let go of the negative memories and emotions so that happiness and joy can fill your soul.

Jesus has already forgiven you. You can forgive yourself, too.

If we confess our sins, he is faithful and just and will forgive us our sins and purify us from all unrighteousness.

I John 1:9

August 9

Plant a tree today.

If you live in a home that has a yard, plant a tree in your own yard. Make it a memorial tree to forgiveness in your life. Every time you see the tree, you will be reminded of the need to forgive others as well as the joy that comes from receiving freedom from your own sins and iniquities. Make this date a "picnic under the tree" date for years to come.

If you do not have a yard, ask a friend or relative if you can plant a tree in their yard. Consider planting a tree in your family's favorite public park or church yard.

If you enjoy learning about plants, visit www.arborday.org. Membership in the Arbor Day Foundation includes ten free trees. This site also includes a guide to trees that thrive in different regions of the nation. There are also suggestions for volunteer opportunities in your city.

August 10

Forgive someone from your past today.

It is not uncommon for people to have things in their past that are huge, things that feel impossible to forgive. Today I encourage you to let go of this thing.

Forgiveness does not mean that you are instantaneously best friends with the person who has offended you. It does not require that a relationship develop after the words are given. Forgive so that you can be released from the pain and burden of carrying it around with you any longer. Forgive so that this pain is not passed down to the next generation.

If the person who comes to your mind is no longer living, write a letter to this person. Express your feelings and forgiveness in words, poetry, art, or lyrics. You can save this letter or burn it when you are done. Regardless what becomes of the page, remove this person's sin from your heart.

Remember, if the person who has offended you has repented of their sins, God has already forgiven that person. God forgives without consulting the offended person first. He will do the same for you, too.

Ask God to forgive your sins against others. Ask God to forgive you for holding on to your resentment and anger toward others as well. Release yourself from this burden today.

August 11

Today let's break down the word "forgiving." There are probably fancy definitions of the term and the concept. My favorite, however, is the word itself: "for" + "giving."

Assignment Whisper is all about giving of yourself, giving your time, energy, personality, character, honesty, integrity, and morals.

Forgiveness is also about giving. It is about giving freedom from past pains, delivering people from grudges, and releasing yourself and others from histories that cannot be changed.

Think today how you can "for give" to others. Who are the specific people in your life that need you to give to them in a way that is new? What can you do that is healing in nature?

Remember, what you do today does not need to be a physical giving. It can be a spiritual or emotional giving. It just needs to be a giving that is for that person's benefit and not your own.

* *Assignment Whisper* *

August 12

Before the summer ends, consider these inspirational book recommendations.

The Jesus I never Knew by Philip Yancey will help you see Jesus in a whole new light. Yancey's observations are thought provoking and motivating. If Jesus is not your best friend already, Yancy's writing presents Jesus in a distinctive manner that will motivate you to invite Jesus over for Sunday brunch.

The Gift of Forgiveness by Charles F. Stanley is another book that will cleanse your heart this summer. There are many books on the market that address the concept of forgiveness. In my opinion, however, Stanley's book dives into the heart of the matter and carries the reader back to the surface for a breath of fresh air.

The Bible is also the ultimate source of information on forgiveness. If you are not familiar with the use of a lexicon for researching in the Bible, ask a pastor or friend to help you learn this skill. You will be very blessed by learning how to study word meanings in the Bible.

August 13

<u>Nail in the Fence</u>
Author Unknown

There once was a little girl who had a bad temper. Her mother gave her a bag of nails and told her that every time she lost her temper, she must hammer a nail into the back of the fence.

The first day the girl had driven 37 nails into the fence. Over the next few weeks, as she learned to control her anger, the number of nails hammered daily gradually dwindled down. She discovered it was easier to hold her temper than to drive those nails into the fence.

Finally the day came when the girl didn't lose her temper at all.

She told her mother about it and the mother suggested that the girl now pull out one nail for each day that she was able to hold her temper.

The days passed and the young girl was finally able to tell her mother that all the nails were gone. The mother took her daughter by the hand and led her to the fence.

She said, "You have done well, my daughter, but look at the holes in the fence. The fence will never be the same. When you say things in anger, they leave a scar just like this one."

You can put a knife in a person and draw it out. It won't matter how many times you say I'm sorry, the wound is still there. A verbal wound is as bad as a physical one.

Please forgive those who have ever left a hole in your fence, and endeavor to not leave holes in anyone else's fence.

* *Assignment Whisper* *

August 14

And be kind one to another, tenderhearted, forgiving one another, just as God in Christ also forgave you.

Ephesians 4:32

Most gifts include decorative paper, a bow, and a card. However, not all gifts can be wrapped in a pretty package. Sometimes gifts are presented in other ways.

Kindness, tenderheartedness, and forgiveness are all gifts that cannot be wrapped in a gift box. Yet they are all gifts that we long to receive. Regardless of the circumstances of our lives, we each desire to receive these gifts. We are all capable of giving these gifts to others, each and every one of us.

Notice the order of the words in the passage above. Forgiveness comes more naturally when proceeded by kindness and a tender heart. When our hearts are hard, they are closed to the idea of forgiveness. When we open our hearts to be kind to others, forgiveness follows.

If you find your heart hesitating when it comes to forgiving others, remember that God also forgave you. If being kind does not inspire forgiveness, recall that forgiveness was given to you through Christ even though you did not deserve it. This will inspire you to make the leap to forgiving others.

August 15

A woman was trying hard to get the ketchup to come out of the jar. During her struggle, the phone rang, and she asked her 4-year-old daughter to answer the phone.

"It's the minister, Mommy," the child said to her mother.

She added, "Mommy can't talk to you right now. She's hitting the bottle."

Check your perception today.

Have you misunderstood someone or something in your life? Are you hearing words without hearing the meaning behind them? Do you need to adjust your thoughts about someone or something?

* *Assignment Whisper* *

August 16

Show some appreciation to a local funeral home director today.

Most funeral home directors lead a hard lifestyle. If the business is in smaller communities, morgues could be miles away. Without a morgue, the funeral director must stop whatever he is doing and attend to the family as soon as a death occurs.

When the business is located in a larger metropolitan areas, it may have a larger staff. This allows each employee to have the guaranty of time off each week. However, larger cities also means more deaths and more funerals.

A funeral director sees some gruesome things at work. He or she also spends the majority of working hours with grieving families, families who may not be feeling pleasant toward each other. The death of a loved one can tear families apart like nothing else can.

Provide a ray of sunshine to a funeral director today. Here are some ideas to brighten his or her day:

- ❖ Take cookies.
- ❖ Send a comic strip in the mail.
- ❖ Write a thank you note. Deliver it in person or put it in the mail.
- ❖ Cut a bouquet of fresh flowers from your garden.
- ❖ Sing cheerful songs with your children.
- ❖ Donate facial tissues. They use these in abundance.
- ❖ Order pizza delivered for lunch.
- ❖ Note your ideas here.

August 17

While cleaning your pantry today, collect any Box Tops for Education that you have.

According to the websites, the Box Tops for Education program began in 1996. In 2008, it reached the $250 million mark in donations. Box Tops for Education is sponsored by General Mills. Most of their products, foods as well as non-food items, contain a Box Top for Education symbol. By collecting these and donating them to your local school, your school can raise money for your child's school or other organization.

Schools also earn money when participants shop from the Box Top website. Many other businesses across the nation partner with General Mills to provide a percentage of sales generated from their site to the school or organization of your choice. Participants register and shop; the companies do the rest.

Visit www.boxtops4education.com to register today. You can begin shopping and find the school of your choice to donate your Box Tops from your pantry. Remember to print free grocery store coupons while you are there.

* *Assignment Whisper* *

August 18

Thank the construction crew at a local public building today.

Chances are high that you have walked past a construction site at some point in your life. Have you ever paid any attention to the men and women working there? Have you ever acknowledged their presence? Yes, I realize that construction workers have a reputation for doing nothing but whistling at pretty girls who walk past, but those building get finished somehow. They must do something besides whistle.

Stop by a building that is under construction today and thank the workers for doing a good job. Let them know that you realize how hard they work and how important their skill is to the community. Remember you are whispering - not whistling!

* *Assignment Whisper* *

August 19

Volunteer at Big Brothers, Big Sisters of America.

Big Brothers Big Sisters matches children ages six through eighteen with mentors in professionally supported one-to-one relationships. Most volunteers spend an average of four hours a month with their little brother or sister. Those four hours can change the life of a participant in ways you cannot imagine.

If you are more comfortable donating money to their cause, their website states that 92.2% of every dollar goes directly to making and supporting matches. This is an impressive number for such a large organization.

If you have a child that you would like to register for the program, the website will provide you details with how to do this.

Visit www.bbbs.org for more information on how to get involved in this fabulous organization.

* *Assignment Whisper* *

August 20

One day, a grandmother was telling her little granddaughter what her own childhood was like.

"We used to skate outside on a pond. I had a swing made from a tire; it hung from a tree in our front yard. We rode our pony. We picked wild raspberries in the woods."

The little girl was wide-eyed, taking this in.

At last she said, "I sure wish I'd gotten to know you sooner!"

Spend some time today with your grandparents. Ask them about their childhood. They have amazing stories to tell. Tell them stories of the wonderful things you remember about them. Let them know that they are still an important and foundational part of your life.

If your grandparents are no longer living, write them a letter telling them how much you miss them. Write about the good times that you had with them. Document everything you can remember about their lives. Record the stories that they told you about their ancestors. Include pictures if you have them.

Share these stories and pictures with your children. Pass them on to the next generation. Keep your grandparents alive through your memories.

August 21

Put an extra big tip in the car wash staff's donation can today.

If you do not frequent a car wash, do it today. Just this once. These people work so hard in all types of weather. Most of them barely earn enough to afford any sort of car of their own. They share tips because they each work on every car that goes through in a given day.

If you cannot afford to give a generous tip, donate what you are able and include a thank you note. Write something that they can share and post on the employee room bulletin board. Make them feel special.

August 22

Acknowledge your local sewage plant staff today.

Consider what your home and your world would look like if there were no sewage plants in your city. What would happen when you flushed your toilet? What would change if every home in America had its own septic system? What if your neighbors did not maintain their septic system? Can you smell the point I am trying to make?

Sewage plants are a necessary part of the infrastructure of American cities. Yet most of us are more comfortable with forgetting that they exist. Someone mans these stations day in and day out so that we do not have to think about them. Someone ensures that our private flushes do not become public health hazards.

Here are some ideas to brighten their day:

❖ Take cookies.
❖ Write a thank you note. Deliver it in person or put it in the mail.
❖ Cut a bouquet of fresh flowers from your garden.
❖ Sing cheerful songs with your children.
❖ Donate air fresheners.
❖ Supply antibacterial wipes.
❖ Order pizza delivered for lunch.
❖ Note your ideas here.

Assignment Whisper

August 23

<u>The Duck and the Devil</u>
Author Unknown

There was a little boy visiting his grandparents on their farm. He was given a slingshot to play with out in the woods. He practiced in the woods; but he could never hit the target. Getting a little discouraged, he headed back for dinner.

As he was walking back he saw Grandma's pet duck. Just out of impulse, he let the slingshot fly, hit the duck square in the head and killed it. He was shocked and grieved! In a panic, he hid the dead duck in the wood pile; only to see his sister watching! Sally had seen it all, but she said nothing.

After lunch the next day Grandma said, "Sally, let's wash the dishes" But Sally said, "Grandma, Johnny told me he wanted to help in the kitchen." Then she whispered to him, "Remember the duck?" So Johnny did the dishes.

Later that day, Grandpa asked if the children wanted to go fishing and Grandma said, "I'm sorry but I need Sally to help make supper."

Sally just smiled and said, "Well that's all right because Johnny told me he wanted to help." She whispered again, "Remember the duck?" So Sally went fishing with Grandpa, and Johnny stayed to help.

After several days of Johnny doing both his chores and Sally's; he finally couldn't stand it any longer.

He came to Grandma and confessed that he had killed the duck.

Grandma knelt down, gave him a hug and said, "Sweetheart, I know. You see, I was standing at the window and I saw the whole thing, but because I love you, I forgave you. I was just wondering how long you would let Sally make a slave of you."

Thought for the day and every day thereafter?

Whatever is in your past, whatever you have done... and the devil keeps throwing it up in your face (lying, cheating, debt, fear, bad habits, hatred, anger, bitterness, etc.)...whatever it is...You need to know that God was standing at the window and He saw the whole thing. He has seen your whole life. He wants you to know that He loves you and that you are forgiven.

He's just wondering how long you will let the devil make a slave of you.

The great thing about God is that when you ask for forgiveness; He not only forgives you, but He forgets. It is by God's grace and mercy that we are saved.

When Jesus died on the cross; he was thinking of you!

August 24

Join in2books today.

This organization matches you with a child who needs encouragement with reading. Participants correspond through the internet or letters. The suggested reading list assists with the selection of material. If you love to read, this is a great way to whisper to a child.

You can also get your own children involved in this group. You can select a child who is the same age as your children. Choose books that your child is reading as well or has an interest in reading. The discussions that you have with your own child will help you to prepare for your conversations with your pen pal about the book.

Visit www.in2books.epals.com/penpal08 for more information and to apply to participate. Background checks are required.

August 25

Do you like animals?

Volunteer to help with animal conservation today. You may enjoy some hands on volunteering that comes from spending time at the local animal shelter, or you may enjoy educating others about wild animals or endangered species.

Here are some ideas to get you started:

❖ Greenpeace - www.greenpeace.org/usa
❖ www.animalconcerns.org
❖ People for the Ethical Treatment of Animals
   www.peta.org/actioncenter
❖ Advocacy for Animal Welfare
   www.apparitionarts.com/animalactivism.html
❖ International Crane Foundation
   www.savingcranes.org

August 26

Pack your suitcase and prepare to relax. Vacation time has arrived.

For some people, those words bring excitement and adventure. Other readers cringe at the thought of leaving home. Business travelers concentrate on meeting agendas more than the relocation process. Whatever the case, hotels lobbies lack the thrill of exploration and the comfort associated with home.

Today's whispering assignment strives to change the personality of hotel lobbies. Plan an activity night at your local hotel or extended stay facility. Certain hotel chains provide evening snacks as well as space for guests to read. Offer your time and energy to entertain the guests and provide a break from the hotel routine.

Some ideas include:
- ❖Organize a karaoke contest.
- ❖Conduct bingo games.
- ❖Teach kazoo lessons.
- ❖Perform songs.
- ❖Promote local events.
- ❖Lead a Bible study or prayer group.
- ❖Host a story hour for the kids.
- ❖Organize a coloring contest for all ages.
- ❖Host an impromptu talent show for all ages.
- ❖Note your ideas here.

Be sure to discuss your plans with the hotel manager before your arrival.

* *Assignment Whisper* *

August 27

Swim for Multiple Sclerosis Association of America.

If you and your family enjoy swimming, use your hobby to benefit this worthy organization. For more information about their swimming events, visit this website: www.msassociation.org.

If you are not a swimmer, there are other ways to support the Multiple Sclerosis organization. Their Dine in Nine fundraisers can be done in any location in a style that suites your tastes.

If you have small children in your family, you could host a Teddy Bear Picnic for MS. Their website suggests this idea for younger children. Let's face it - we all love teddy bears!

Older children might enjoy hosting a miniature golf tournament as a fundraiser. Gamers would enjoy hosting a QuizMS event. These events can be held in any location of your choosing. They are all fun and unique ways to raise both funds and awareness about MS.

Visit www.msassociation.org for a variety of creative ideas about serving this organization.

August 28

The Cracked Pot
Author Unknown

A water bearer in India had two large pots, each hung on each end of a pole which he carried across his neck. One of the pots had a crack in it, and while the other pot was perfect and always delivered a full portion of water at the end of the long walk from the stream to the master's house, the cracked pot arrived only half full. For a full two years this went on daily, with the bearer delivering only one and a half pots full of water in his master's house. Of course, the perfect pot was proud of its accomplishments, perfect to the end for which it was made. But the poor cracked pot was ashamed of its own imperfection, and miserable that it was able to accomplish only half of what it had been made to do.

After two years of what it perceived to be a bitter failure, it spoke to the water bearer one day by the stream. "I am ashamed of myself, and I want to apologize to you." "Why?" asked the bearer. "What are you ashamed of?" "I have been able, for these past two years, to deliver only half my load because this crack in my side causes water to leak out all the way back to your master's house. Because of my flaws, you have to do all of this work, and you don't get full value from your efforts," the pot said.

The water bearer felt sorry for the old cracked pot, and in his compassion he said, "As we return to the master's house, I want you to notice the beautiful flowers along the path." Indeed, as they went up the hill, the old cracked pot took notice of the sun warming the beautiful wild flowers on the side of the path, and this cheered it some.

But at the end of the trail, it still felt bad because it had leaked half its load, and so again it apologized to the bearer for its failure. The bearer said to the pot, "Did you notice that there were flowers only on your side of your path, but not on the other pot's side? That's because I have always known about your flaw, and I took advantage of it. I planted flower seeds on your side of the path, and every day while we walk back from the stream, you've watered them. For two years I have been able to pick these beautiful flowers to decorate my master's table. Without you being just the way you are, he would not have this beauty to grace his house."

Each of us has our own unique flaws. We're all cracked pots. But if we will allow it, the Lord will use our flaws to grace His Father's table. In God's great economy, nothing goes to waste. So as we seek ways to minister together, and as God calls you to the tasks He has appointed for you, don't be afraid of your flaws. Acknowledge them, and allow Him to take advantage of them, and you, too, can be the cause of beauty in His pathway.

Go out boldly, knowing that in our weakness we find His strength, and that "In Him every one of God's promises is a Yes". For with God, nothing shall be impossible.

Luke 1:37

August 29

Volunteer at your local food bank or soup kitchen today.

Many people think of this idea during the holidays. However, we need to remember that people get hungry every day of the year. The need does not go away simply because there is no holiday.

If you are not aware of the locations of your community soup kitchens, contact your library, church, or community center. They may host meals or be able to direct you to a convenient location. Even if you live in a small town, the chances are high that there is at least one group that feeds the homeless on a regular basis.

Food banks are also amazingly educational when it comes to whispering to the hungry people in your community. While food banks might appear to be nothing more than a grocery store with a twist, you will be amazed at what you can learn about hunger and those in need by volunteering there.

You will also learn about the businesses and corporations in your area that support the food bank. Sending these companies a thank you note demonstrates that you appreciate their involvement in the community. Acknowledging public awareness of corporate participation provides incentive to continue.

Put on a hair net and your best smile. Volunteering at the soup kitchen does not require cooking skills. All you need is a serving spoon and an open heart to impact someone's day.

* *Assignment Whisper* *

August 30

Pray for your state's board of education today.

Schools across the nation are preparing to open their doors. The planning is over. The decisions are made. Although the work of the school board is by no means over, the fruits of their labor are about to be tried and tested.

If you live in a small community, find the names of your local school board members. Write them thank you notes for the service they provide to the community. Attend a school board meeting to express your appreciation. Take cookies!

Whether you live in a large city or small community, your local school board members are governed by the state's Board of Education. Pray for the members of the state board as well as the local board. The internet will probably provide a mailing address for the commissioner. Write a thank you note to him or her and ask him to share it with the other members of the board.

If your children are in private school or are homeschooled, remember that not everyone has that choice for their children. The services provided by our public schools are valuable, and those who run the public school deserve our appreciation.

* *Assignment Whisper* *

August 31

You will never plough a field
if you only turn it over in your mind.

Irish Proverb

How are you doing with your whispering? Have you made it this far in this devotional without doing anything but thinking about the ideas and suggestions? Have you been inspired for a matter of moments but not enough to actually do anything?

If that is the case, today is the day to change your ways. Forget about the fact that you have not actually whispered all year. Start now. Make a commitment to yourself to whisper during the remainder of the year.

You may remember one idea that moved you, or you may find that you need to keep reading to discover the whisper that speaks to your heart. Whatever the case, commit to yourself now that you will do more than turn it over in your mind.

If you have been whispering and loving it, consider your field ploughed! Sit down with a mug of Irish coffee, and rejoice in how good it has felt to whisper.

* *Assignment Whisper* *

September 1

Summer is almost over, and fall will be arriving soon. In some parts of the country, the trees are already turning colors, and people are buying adhesive bandages in preparation for raking blisters.

God, in His infinite wisdom, knew that the earth needed its rest. Just like people need a break, the land also needs a time of respite between harvests.

In the New Testament, "rest" can be translated as, "to cause or permit one to cease from any movement or labor in order to recover and collect his strength." It can also mean, "to keep quiet, of calm and patient expectation."

Webster defines "rest" as a freedom from activity or labor. Webster also defines "rest" as peace of mind or spirit.

As fall arrives, focus on rest as peace of mind. Enjoy the patient expectation that comes from God's love. As you whisper to others this month, project a feeling of peace and expectation to them. Let them enjoy the rest that is inherent to the autumn season.

The Lord replied, "My Presence will go with you, and I will give you rest."

Exodus 33:14

[Jesus said] Come to me, all you who are weary and burdened, and I will give you rest.

Matthew 11:28

September 2

Arrange time for your spouse to rest today. Make it possible for his or her day to be more restful than it has been for a long time.

Before he or she comes home, do these things:

❖ Complete chores for him or her.

❖ Forget about daily chores for one day.

❖ Burn your list of "honey do" items.

❖ Prepare a favorite dinner.

❖ Make a plate of comfort food snacks.

❖ Unplug the phone.

❖ Hide the television remotes.

❖ Coach the kids to be quiet and peaceful.

❖ Give him or her your undivided attention from the moment he or she walks in the door. Spend all of your energy setting the stage for a restful reprise and ensuring the evening stays that way.

❖ Enjoy your spouse and rest together.

* *Assignment Whisper* *

September 3

Plan a party day for the kids. Today it is your children's turn to rest from their chores. It will not hurt for nothing to be done for one day.

If today is a weekend or holiday, spend the day in your pajamas. Get a family-friendly movie to watch together. Order in pizza so that you do not have to cook. Spend time doing the things that your children would consider restful.

Some other ideas might include:

❖Enjoy a picnic in the backyard or local park.
❖Take a trip to the mall.
❖Make homemade ice cream or snow cones.
❖Plan a trip to the swimming pool (possibly the last of the summer.)
❖Organize a scrapbooking day.
❖Create a city in the driveway with sidewalk chalks.
❖Improve your suntan in the backyard.
❖Redistribute the household chores before school begins.

If you do not have children of your own, consider borrowing some relatives for the day, or spend the day with your match from Big Brother, Big Sisters of America.

September 4

Today is your day to rest. Do something for yourself. Let your entire family know that you are taking a day of respite. Inform them that you will not be entertaining requests for the entire day. The day is yours. Let them wait on you!

Everyone has their own idea of what is restful. You may decide that the most restful thing is to tackle your unfinished "to do" list. Maybe a manicure and a yummy chocolate bar is all it takes to make you feel revived and alive. That cruise vacation that tempts you cannot be done in 24 hours, so be realistic.

To some people, peaceful days include as many people as possible. Others would rather be alone to rejuvinate themselves. Whichever you decide, plan ahead so that you can achieve your perfect state of relaxation.

Remember that today's goal is relaxation, peace of mind, and quiet expectation for tomorrow. Set the scene and enjoy the event!

* *Assignment Whisper* *

September 5

Bookmark the following site on your computer and commit to visit it daily: www.thehungersite.com/clicktogive
This site has tabs for these six causes:
❖ hunger
❖ breast cancer
❖ child health
❖ literacy
❖ rain forest
❖ animal rescue

By clicking on these six sites, the sponsors make a donation to that particular cause. All you do is click. You can click daily.

The website also details ways to donate to these six causes. In addition, you will find a list of sponsors for the cause that is closest to your heart.

If one of these causes is a passion of yours, write a thank you note to the sponsors of that particular website. Encourage your friends to support these businesses, too.

September 6

Take your best friend to lunch today. Tell him or her thank you for being such a good friend. Show your appreciate and gratitude for the relationship.

Not everyone in the world is fortunate enough to have a best friend. Some people relocate too often to develop lasting relationships. Other people exhaust their energies at work and do not have any liveliness left for friendships. Men in particular seem less inclined to bond outside of work.

Whether it is a work associate, a best friend since childhood, or a friend who has stood by you during tough times, spend some quality time with that person today. Do everything you can to eliminate any possible interruptions during your time together. Make it a point to verbally express how much you appreciate that person and their presence in your life.

If your best friend does not live close to you, set aside some time to call that person. Perhaps you can arrange a time in advance when you can both talk uninterrupted, or write a letter that he or she can save for years to come.

Let the special people in your life know how much their friendship means to you today.

* *Assignment Whisper* *

September 7

Today's whispering assignment is a silent task.

Give everyone a rest from your whining and complaining today. Resolve to speak positivity or not at all.

For some of you this will be a very easy assignment. There are still Pollyanna personalities in the world who can easily see the bright side of any situation. If you are one of these people, congratulations! Still be mindful of your speech today in case you are letting more slip out than you realize.

If you are a whiner, today will be difficult for you. You are giving everyone in your life a rest from your negative speak patterns. Do not complain about anything at all today. Hold your tongue until you can phrase your thoughts in a positive way. If you cannot think of a cheerful way to say what you are thinking, then do not say anything at all. Trust me, no one will miss knowing what is making you unhappy.

Most of this devotional has been about giving or doing for others. Today's task still does follow that theme. Today you are giving a respite to others. I think you will enjoy it and the reaction you receive from others as well.

* *Assignment Whisper* *

September 8

During a visit to the mental asylum, a visitor asked the Director what is the criteria that defines a patient to be institutionalized.

"Well," said the Director, "we fill up a bathtub, we offer a teaspoon, a teacup, and a bucket to the patient and ask the patient to empty the bathtub." Okay, here's your test:

1. Would you use the spoon?
2. Would you use the teacup?
3. Would you use the bucket?

"Oh, I understand," said the visitor. "A normal person would choose the bucket as it is larger than the spoon or the cup."

"Noooo," answered the Director. "A normal person would pull the plug."

What things in your life are you doing the hard way? Simplify your life in any way that you can. Do things the easy way so that you have more time to rest and whisper.

September 9

LIFTING WEIGHTS
by Monique Nicole Fox

Come to God
all that are weary
and burdened with life's weights
let God lift you from dire straights

Come to God
all that are overwhelmed and stressed
let God lift you from the entire mess

Come to God
all that are in need of guidance and help
let God lift you out of that circumstance

Come to God
all that are confused and in turmoil
let God lift you out of the muddy waters, filth
  and quick sands soil

Come to God
all that are run down and tired
let God save you before you drown
You will find Him the best weight lifter in town

**[Jesus said] Come to me, all you who are weary
and burdened, and I will give you rest. Take my
yoke upon you and learn from me, for I am gentle
and humble in heart, and you will find rest for
your souls.**

Matthew 11:28-29

* *Assignment Whisper* *

September 10

Today remember the staff at a blood donation center.

Hopefully you donated blood earlier in the year and have continued to do that as you are able. Perhaps you have met some staff and know them by name. If you have continued to donate blood throughout the year, you realize how dedicated these people are and the value of the job they do. Each unit of blood saves three lives within 24 hours of your donation. The staff at the centers are part of that miracle, too.

Here are some ideas to brighten their day:
- ❖ Take homemade cookies.
- ❖ Sing a cheerful song with your children.
- ❖ Donate a bottle of hand lotion; gloves can dry the skin.
- ❖ Order pizza delivered for lunch.
- ❖ Contribute magazines for the waiting room.
- ❖ Donate children's toys for the play area.
- ❖ Draw or paint a picture for the wall.
- ❖ Supply a box of pens.
- ❖ Note your ideas here.

September 11

Today is a day of rest from anger and hatred.

Most Americans remember exactly what they were doing when they learned of the terrorist attacks of September 11, 2001. The feelings of disbelief, shock, and pain are still alive in our hearts and minds. The imagines shown on television remain fresh in our memories.

In September 2001, my family was living in a multi-cultural neighborhood. Before the attacks, residents of all nationalities were outside on a daily basis chatting with their neighbors. Our kids played together at the community pool. We traded keys to our homes in case of emergencies. We all knew each other's names and were on friendly terms.

Immediately after the attacks, all of that community spirit died. Residents from one nationality no longer spoke to neighbors from other countries. Kids stopped riding their bikes in the cul-de-sac. Bunco groups reviewed their membership.

While it is good to remember what happened that day, it is also good to remember that not every foreigner you meet is a terrorist. We do not need to carry the hatred to the point of closing our hearts to other human beings.

Today as you remembering the attacks, let go of the hatred and anger toward people. Let your memories of the events focus on the terrorists, not the nationality of those people. We do not want people of other nations to judge us according to what they see on daytime soap operas. Let's not judge them by the actions of a select group of terrorists.

September 12

Volunteer at Ronald McDonald House today.

The Ronald McDonald houses provide a home away from home for families whose children are in hospitals for long periods of time. They also provide family rooms inside hospitals for family members to rest and regroup while their children receive medical services. Ronald McDonald Care Mobiles travel to children who need medical attention but are unable to journey to the hospital.

According to their website, Ronald McDonald houses can be found in 52 countries as of 2008. There is even a 31-bedroom house at the Vatican.

Visit www.rmhc.com for more information about their services as well as ways to get involved in this organization. You will find more than just fries and floppy red shoes.

Some ways to get involved include:

❖Volunteer your time and talents.

❖Donate toys, food, magazines, or house wares.

❖Collect pop tabs.

❖Contribute your change at McDonald's.

❖Purchase a USA Today the next time you dine at McDonalds. In-restaurant sales of USA Today are all donated to RMHC.

❖Draw or paint a picture for the wall of a hospital Family Room.

❖Host a fundraiser to educate others as well as raise funds for RMHC.

❖Note your ideas here.

* *Assignment Whisper* *

September 13

Contact your local Welcome Wagon representative to see how you can volunteer with this organization.

Welcome Wagons have been around for many years. They welcome people into the neighborhood. They promote area businesses and assist families in connecting with area resources. Their missions may vary from city to city, but their overall objective remains the building of communities.

Some groups welcome people into the neighborhood when they first arrive. Other groups provide more social activities and opportunities for women to meet other women and families to form friendships with other families. Some groups focus on that one-time call while others will meet with you several times to ensure that you are settled in your new home.

Some ways to get involved include:

❖Volunteer to visit people who move into your neighborhood.

❖Donate small gifts to include in the welcome baskets from you personally or from your business.

❖Host a welcome party for the new family on the block.

❖Cook supper for a new family on that first night in their new home when their kitchen is still packed.

❖Invite the children for a play date to provide the parents time to unpack.

❖Compile a list of "kids eat free" restaurants in your area for the new family.

❖Note your ideas here.

* *Assignment Whisper* *

September 14

Give yourself rest from the clutter in your closet today. Donate professional clothing to a halfway house or homeless shelter.

Find a group or organization in your community that assists people in their job search. These people generally do not have enough money to purchase new clothing for interviews. Most everyone has one or two outfits in their closet that are still in perfect condition but are never worn. Put these outfits to good use today. Donate them to someone who can use them to get a new job and begin a new life.

Other ideas include:

❖Volunteer at the local shelter to sort and organize donations.

❖Donate clothes hangers.

❖Volunteer to take donations home and launder them.

❖Offer to help others select outfits for interviews. You do not need a well-developed fashion sense to encourage someone as they put together the perfect outfit.

❖Take your video camera and conduct practice interviews with the residents.

❖Drive a woman to the mall and let the ladies at the beauty counter give her a free make-over.

❖Note your ideas here.

* *Assignment Whisper* *

September 15

Donate magazines to doctor or dentist office today.

The topic of the magazine does not matter. Any reading material is appreciated by people waiting for an appointment time. Reading medical advertising magazines is no fun for anyone.

Sort through the stack of magazines on your coffee table and put the magazines in your car. If you drive past your doctor or dentist office on a regular basis, donate the magazines today. It will only take a minute to leave them with the receptionist.

If your pediatric dentist shows movies to the patients, ask your children to contribute one of their old movies. If your kids have books that they have outgrown, these are a good idea as well.

If you are donating magazines that you received in the mail, remember to remove your mailing address before donating them.

September 16

Stress Management
Author Unknown

A lecturer, when explaining stress management to an audience, raised a glass of water and asked, "How heavy is this glass of water?"

Answers called out ranged from 20g to 500g.

The lecturer replied, "The absolute weight doesn't matter. It depends on how long you try to hold it. If I hold it for a minute, that's not a problem. If I hold it for an hour, I'll have an ache in my right arm. If I hold it for a day, you'll have to call an ambulance. In each case, it's the same weight, but the longer I hold it, the heavier it becomes."

He continued, "And that's the way it is with stress management. If we carry our burdens all the time, sooner or later, as the burden becomes increasingly heavy, we won't be able to carry on. As with the glass of water, you have to put it down for a while and rest before holding it again. When we're refreshed, we can carry on with the burden."

"So, before you return home tonight, put the burden of work down. Don't carry it home. You can pick it up tomorrow. Whatever burdens you're carrying now, let them down for a moment if you can."

Live simply. Love generously. Care deeply. Speak kindly. Leave the rest to God.

September 17

Volunteer to be a docent at your local museum.

Docents are common at many museums and usually volunteers. Museums are a great place to meet fascinating people. Patrons to the museum appreciate the expertise and attention they receive from the docents. A trip to the museum is always more fun when you learn about what you are seeing from someone who has a passion for the exhibit.

Contact your local museum and review their schedule. If they currently do not have anything that interests you, ask what exhibits are coming later in the year. Plan now to be a docent in the near future.

You do not necessarily need expertise in a topic before becoming a docent. The museum with provide you with information to study. You will learn as much as you teach.

September 18

Volunteer with the Salvation Army today.

The Salvation Army is far more than red buckets at Christmas time manned by bell-ringing Santas. They provide a variety of services throughout the year.

The Salvation Army's Missing Person Service strives to reunite people in families who wish to find each other. This organization has produced some of the most outstanding brass bands in the world. The Salvation Army Adult Rehabilitation Center ministries in the United States provide an in-residence rehabilitation program with a focus on basic necessities. Services are also provided to survivors of natural disasters as well as the elderly of our nation throughout the year. The Salvation Army works to eliminate human trafficking. In addition, they maintain community serve centers for military personnel, children's programs, and prison ministries.

Visit www.salvationarmyusa.org for ways that you can volunteer with this organization.

* *Assignment Whisper* *

September 19

Dad's Brownies
Author Unknown

Last week, I walked into my office to find a sandwich bag on my desk containing three chewy, tasty, homemade chocolate brownies. Some thoughtful and anonymous person who knew my love for tasty homemade brownies had placed them there, along with a hand written short story.

I immediately sat down and began eating the first chewy, tasty, homemade brownie as I read the following story:

Two teenagers asked their father if they could go to the theater to watch a movie that all their friends had seen. After reading some reviews about the movie on the internet, he denied their request.

"Aw dad, why not?" they complained. "It's rated PG-13, and we're both older than thirteen!"

Dad replied, "Because that movie contains nudity and portrays immorality as being normal and acceptable behavior."

"But Dad, those are just very small parts of the movie! That's what our friends who've seen it have told us. The movie is two hours long and those scenes are just a few minutes of the total film! It's based on a true story, and good triumphs over evil, and there are other redeeming themes like courage and self-sacrifice. Even the movie review web sites say that!"

"My answer is 'no,' and that is my final answer. You are welcome to stay home tonight, invite some of your friends over, and watch one of the good videos we have in our home collection.

But you will not go and watch that film. End of discussion."

The two teenagers walked dejectedly into the family room and slumped down on the couch. As they sulked, they were surprised to hear the sounds of their father preparing something in the kitchen. They soon recognized the wonderful aroma of brownies baking in the oven, and one of the teenagers said to the other, "Dad must be feeling guilty, and now he's going to try to make it up to us with some fresh brownies. Maybe we can soften him with lots of praise when he brings them out to us and persuade him to let us go to that movie after all."

About that time I began eating the second brownie from the sandwich bag and wondered if there was some connection to the brownies I was eating and the brownies in the story. I kept reading.

The teens were not disappointed. Soon their father appeared with a plate of warm brownies, which he offered to his kids. They each took one.

Then their father said, "Before you eat, I want to tell you something: I love you both so much."

The teenagers smiled at each other with knowing glances. Dad was softening.

"That is why I've made these brownies with the very best ingredients. I've made them from scratch. Most of the ingredients are even organic. The best organic flour. The best free-range eggs. The best organic sugar. Premium vanilla and chocolate."

The brownies looked mouthwatering, and the teens began to become a little impatient with their dad's long speech.

"But I want to be perfectly honest with you. There is one ingredient I added that is not usually found in brownies. I got that ingredient from our own back yard. But you needn't worry, because I only added the tiniest bit of that ingredient to your brownies. The amount of the portion is practically insignificant. So go ahead, take a bite and let me know what you think."

"Dad, would you mind telling us what that mystery ingredient is before we eat?"

"Why? The portion I added was so small. Just a teaspoonful. You won't even taste it."

"Come on, Dad, just tell us what that ingredient is."

"Don't worry! It is organic, just like the other ingredients."

"Dad!"

"Well, OK, if you insist. That secret ingredient is fresh organic...dog poop."

I immediately stopped chewing that second brownie, and I spit it out into the wastebasket by my desk. I continued reading, now fearful of the paragraphs that still remained.

Both teens instantly dropped their brownies back on the plate and began inspecting their fingers with horror.

"DAD! Why did you do that? You've tortured us by making us smell those brownies cooking for the last half hour, and now you tell us that you added dog poop! We can't eat these brownies!"

"Why not? The amount of dog poop is very small compared to the rest of the ingredients. It won't hurt you. It's been cooked right along with the other ingredients. You won't even taste it.

It has the same consistency as the brownies. Go ahead and eat!"

"No, Dad...NEVER!"

"And that is the same reason I won't allow you to go watch that movie. You won't tolerate a little dog poop in your brownies, so why should you tolerate a little immorality in your movies? We pray that God will not lead us unto temptation, so how can we in good conscience entertain ourselves with something that will imprint a sinful image in our minds that will lead us into temptation long after we first see it?"

I discarded what remained of the second brownie as well as the entire untouched third brownie. What had been irresistible a minute go had become detestable. And only because of the very slim chance that what I was eating was slightly polluted. (Surely it wasn't...but I couldn't convince myself.)

What a good lesson about purity! Why do we tolerate any sin? On the day of the Passover, the Israelites were commanded to remove every bit of leaven from their homes.

Sin is like leaven - a little bit leavens the whole lump (1 Corinthians 5:6,7). Faith and sin don' t mix.

What are you digesting? Are you putting things in your heart and body that edify? Does your heart feel rested and revived from the things you ingest? If not, reevaluate what needs to be included in your spiritual diet to provide rest to your body and soul.

* *Assignment Whisper* *

September 20

Volunteer at the Shriner's Hospital.

A few years ago I had the opportunity to assist a family whose son had been burned over 95 % of his body. The Shriner's learned of his situation on the news and immediately arrived to help. They flew him and his family to the Shriner's Hospital that best served his medical needs. They provided housing for his mother. They arranged air and ground transportation at no cost to the family. They cared for the family as well as for the child without charging them a penny. It was amazing.

I later learned that the hospital was manned by volunteers at almost every station except doctors and nurses. The people who flew patients from their home to the hospital were volunteers. The drivers who provided transportation from the airport to the hospital were volunteers. The staff manning the front desk were all volunteers. It brought such joy to my heart to see what the dedication of volunteers can provide to these children and families in need.

Visit this website www.shrinershq.org/Hospitals/Main/ to see how you can be part of this volunteer team.

September 21

Send a card to a hospital patient today.

It is common for hospital websites to provide a way for you to send cards to patients that you know. This hospital goes one step further and allows you to send "random acts of kindness" to a stranger.

Bookmark this page today and visit it often: www.meriter.com/ecard/ecard.htm.

This website allows you to send an anonymous card to a pediatric patient, an elderly hospital patient, or a patient chosen by the hospital staff. Your name and contact information are not included in the card. You can include any information or message you like in the text portion, but the hospital does not reveal your identity.

Investigate your local hospital's policy of ecards. If you have the expertise, consider designing a website option for your hospital to include this feature. If the hospital is already delivering ecards to patients, all it would take is adding the option of "random acts of kindness" to their website.

* *Assignment Whisper* *

September 22

Volunteer at the local YMCA today.

The YMCA is more than a sports center. There are many other classes and programs offered by the YMCA's that are designed to build strong individuals, bond families, and shape communities. Their services provide a physical location to develop strong emotional and spiritual individuals of all ages.

Visit www.ymca.net for more information.

Some volunteer ideas include:

❖Teach a class. Talk to the director now to teach a class in January.

❖Assist in a current class. Every teacher can use an extra pair of hands in the classroom.

❖Sponsor or scholarship a child.

❖Provide water bottles to an exercise class.

❖Assist with a fundraiser.

❖Plan a holiday party for the staff.

❖Offer accounting or clerical support.

❖Note your ideas here.

* *Assignment Whisper* *

September 23

The apostles gathered around Jesus and reported to him all they had done and taught. Then, because so many people were coming and going that they did not even have a chance to eat, he said to them, "Come with me by yourselves to a quiet place and get some rest."

Mark 6:30-31

It was not unusual for Jesus to seek solitude. His ministry was about people. Yet he still took the time to have private moments to revive his soul. He encouraged his disciples to do the same.

In the account told by Mark in the passage above, the disciples had just returned from ministering to people in places apart from Jesus. They assembled to share with Jesus all that had happened while they were apart. Jesus encouraged them to rest in a quiet place after their work.

Rest is an important part of whispering to others. From the beginning of time, taking a break from work was part of the plan. God rested from His work of creation and established the Sabbath. As shown by Jesus' example to his disciples, God has not abandoned that idea over the years.

Remind yourself today of the value of rest while working. A weary worker is not an inspiration to others.

* *Assignment Whisper* *

September 24

In the theme of rest, the book recommendation for this month is the Yada Yada Prayer Group series by Neta Jackson.

There are seven books in this series. They are all easy reads and well worth the time. The characters will inspire you and encourage your whispering in ways you cannot imagine. Their lives will leap off the page and touch your heart.

While the Yada Yada Prayer Group may be best suited for women, the men are not forgotten. Dave Jackson has also written books for the men to be involved in the Yada movement. *Harry Bentley's Second Chance* will get you started on the journey. From there, you will be hooked!

Visit www.daveneta.com for summaries of the books and ordering information. You will be pleased that you did.

September 25

Check out www.firefighterministries.com today. This organization is dedicated to "Protecting and promoting the spiritual, mental, and physical well-being of emergency service workers everywhere." Most of their volunteers work online, serving the ministry through virtual means. Other volunteers spend time at fire stations. Volunteers must be 18 years or older, but a wide variety of talents are used by this group. Their website contains a wealth of information for public servants as well as those interested in supporting them.

If supporting fire fighters is your passion, visit this site for Volunteer Fire Fighters for other ways to serve these brave men and women who work tirelessly for our communities: www.volunteerfd.org/.

September 26

Encourage your friends to rest today.

We all have friends who are routinely stressed by their lives. Some people never embrace the idea of rest and relaxation. There are busy people all over the nation who are spinning their wheels in their frenzied activities. They accomplish nothing beyond sharing their stress with those who are close to them.

Loan an inspirational book to these friends today, and invite their kids over for the afternoon. Select a book recommended in this devotional to share with them. Perhaps they enjoy reading but do not make the time to visit the library or book store. Maybe they forget to give themselves permission to escape into the characters of a engaging novel.

Give your friends an afternoon of rest. Provide a few hours for them to experience the joy of doing nothing. Help them to understand how important it is to take a break from regular chores. Show them how much energy can be obtained by doing nothing for a few hours. Whisper the gift of rest to your friends. Everyone will benefit.

* *Assignment Whisper* *

September 27

Volunteer to clean the football or softball field after a game today.

If you have ever been to a football game, you have probably noticed that people leave a mess in the stands. Someone has to deal with the mess. If you live in an area that has resources, the person cleaning the stadium may be paid staff. However, in many places, these people are volunteers.

Find your local little league schedule or high school football team's calendar. Mark your calendar for a day you can attend the game and clean up following the game. Even if there is paid staff to do this job, designate a section of the stadium that you and your friends and family will clear. Take your own trash bags and gloves. Make it a contest to see who can collect the most trash.

You may want to talk to the local school board or community center to develop a program of "adopt bleachers" similar to "adopt a highway" program. Contact the leaders of local support groups to encourage them to adopt a section of the stadium for one game or an entire season. Businesses will benefit from the advertising provided by their efforts. Individuals will have a sense of ownership and involvement in their local teams.

Assignment Whisper *

September 28

Become a pen pal to an orphan today.

This website will help you get started: www.theorphanfoundation.org.

There are currently 143 million orphans in the world. Imagine how many of those children will turn 18 years old this year and be forced to leave the only home they have ever known. Young children have no one to tuck them into bed at night. Older children may begin adult life with no family to support them. All of these children need your time and love.

The Orphan Foundation has many options for volunteering. Some ideas include:

❖Hands on work in the orphanage.

❖Fundraising.

❖Grant writing.

❖Chefs for Cherubs project.

❖Kids4Kids program.

❖Delivering supplies to orphanages across the globe.

If your community has an orphanage, contact the director to see how you can volunteer there. Ask if your children can spend time with the children, too. If you cannot volunteer in the center, ask how you can work with their publicity department or assist fundraising efforts.

* *Assignment Whisper* *

September 29

Give your parents a day of rest today.

As our parents age, the chores of life become more difficult to complete. Those tasks that used to be accomplished without a second thought are now the source of procrastination. The older we get, the more energy we need to accomplish those things that used to be so effortless.

Give your parents a day of rest by doing these tasks for them today. Plan to spend the day with them doing those little things around their house that are not getting done. Perhaps they need a trip to the grocery store to restock the pantry. Maybe light bulbs need changing in hard to reach places. Checkbooks need balancing or leaves need raking. Whatever it is, help your parents today. Take your children and make it a party.

If your parents are in an assisted living center or nursing home, there may still be little things that are on their mind. Help them write a letter to a friend or redecorate their room. Take some new books they would enjoy. Make new placemats to decorate their lunch table.

If your parents are no longer living, help an elderly relative or neighbor today. Even if that person has family of their own to help them, it is sometimes easier to accept help from a stranger than from family. Give them a time of rest from the worry of asking for help by offering.

* *Assignment Whisper* *

September 30

I will lie down and sleep in peace, for you alone, O Lord, make me dwell in safety.

Psalm 4:8

Read that verse again aloud. Can't you just feel God's arms wrapped around you? Feel the comfort in the safety of His embrace - comfort to the point of peaceful sleep. How beautiful!

Few people are able to sleep in peace when they do not feel safe. Worry and fear can stop anyone from a restful slumber. Knowing that we are safe and protected makes all the difference in the world.

With God, we have that safety. He provides shelter and His hedge of protection so that our hearts and souls can relax and be restored to Him.

Sleep in God's safety. Live your life in a way that allows others to do the same.

* *Assignment Whisper* *

October 1

Today we will whisper appreciation.

Tell God that you appreciate Him today. You may decide to do this through prayer, attending a worship service, or serving others. However you decide to show your appreciation, stay focused on it throughout your entire day.

Appreciation can be expressed through praising God for who He is as well as for all that He has done for you.

In Old Testament times, the people demonstrated their appreciation to God by observing rituals, offering sacrifices, and celebrating festivals.

Moses and the Israelites sang songs of praise to God. Here is an example of their lyrics:

The Lord is my strength and my song; he has become my salvation. He is my God, and I will praise him, my father's God, and I will exalt him.
Exodus 15:2

In New Testament times, we are instructed to praise God through our relationships with other people as well as through worship and song.

Accept one another, then, just as Christ accepted you, in order to bring praise to God.
Romans 15:7

Spend time today whispering appreciate to God for all that He has done in your life.

* *Assignment Whisper* *

October 2

Today is appreciation of your spouse day.

Make a list of all of your spouse's great qualities. Write down everything that you love about him or her. You may decide to make a list, draw a picture, write a poem, or set your feelings to words. Professional artistic talent is not required. All that is necessary is a purity of heart for your spouse.

Share this list with your sweetheart. Even if you have told them these things before, it is always fun to hear them again. Everyone appreciates hearing love from their spouse.

If you are not married, make a list of the attributes that you hope to find in your future spouse. Develop a clear picture in your heart of how it feels to appreciate your spouse. Practice now so that expressing appreciation for your future spouse comes naturally after you say, "I do."

* Assignment Whisper *

October 3

Today, appreciate your children.

If you have more than one child, make individual projects. Do not lump each child's bonding time together. Express your appreciation for them in a way that is personal and exceptional. Outline their outstanding qualities and what you love about each of them.

Do your best to make this list include qualities of who your children are as people, not necessarily about the things they do. Anyone can take out the trash. The focus is that your child remembered trash day out of his or her dedication to the family. Record those personality characteristics that are unique to that person.

If you do not have children, apply today's whispering to a niece or nephew. Ask your siblings if you can borrow their kids for a day to share the fabulous traits that you see in them.

* *Assignment Whisper* *

October 4

Today is family appreciation day.

Tell each of your family members (parents, siblings, aunts, uncles, cousins, etc.) one thing that they have done for you that you appreciate. You may have one relative in mind that needs some extra encouragement at this point in their life. Perhaps you want to focus on that person for today, but do not forget the rest of your family before the month is complete. Everyone deserves to hear what you appreciate about them as people.

Even if you have thanked them before, do it again. Your admiration will still be appreciated because you remembered the event again.

If possible do this in person or through a phone call. Notes are nice, but the personal touch is better.

* *Assignment Whisper* *

October 5

Today we will explore the definition of the word "appreciation."

Webster's dictionary defines this word as:

1a. to grasp the nature, worth, quality, or the significance of

1b. to value or admire highly

1c. to judge with heightened perception or the understanding: be fully aware of

1d. to recognize with gratitude

2. to increase the value of

Interestingly enough, the Bible does not use the term "appreciation" in most translations. Some of the more modern versions that paraphrase the Bible use the word, but the traditional versions use other expressions for this concept. They use words like love, charity, praise, and worship.

When we apply appreciation in our own lives, we should also be focused on praise and gratitude. Is that what God sees in your heart when you praise Him?

* *Assignment Whisper* *

October 6

Contact the local chapter of the United Way for a source of places to volunteer today.

The United Way is an international organization that works with individuals, corporations, and community organizations to meet the needs of the community it serves. By combining resources and working cooperatively, more people can benefit from the generosity of the donations.

Most cities have their own chapter. You can easily find contact information for the group closest to you on the internet or through your local library. For information on United Way International, visit www.uwint.org.

United Way agencies use a wide variety of talent and resources to meet the needs of the community. If you are feeling insecure about your ability to contribute, this is a great organization to help you find your volunteering niche.

Appreciate your community's resources and the willingness of your neighbors and businesses to support the public.

* *Assignment Whisper* *

October 7

Today is appreciation for languages day.

If you are bilingual, volunteer as a translator. Remember that American Sign Language (ASL) counts as a language that needs translators as well. If you read Braille, your services can also be used in a variety of organizations.

If you do not speak a foreign language, consider teaching English as a Second Language (ESL) classes. People learning English need practice developing their new skills. Students of all ages who are learning English can be found at the local library, community college, public schools, and private schools. You do not need to be a trained teacher to assist with translation services. You just need to donate a few hours of your time.

Some organizations need translation of printed materials. Often times you can do these services at home or online.

Appreciate the gift of communication today as you volunteer to interpret a foreign language or assist with ESL classes. While whispering is not always verbal, but it can be translated!

October 8

Sow an act,
   and you reap a habit;
sow a habit,
   and you reap a character;
sow a character,
   and you reap a destiny.

George Dana Boardman

What are you sowing today? Are you sowing acts, habits, or character? What do you need to change in your life so that you are sowing destiny?

Communication is an amazing gift. However, if it is not used properly, it can become a weapon instead of a tool.

Check your sowing today as you whisper and communicate to others. What are you planting?

October 9

Donate to St. Jude's Hospital today.

According to their website, St. Jude's Hospital was founded by Danny Thomas in 1962. Since then, more than 20,000 children from across the United States and 70 foreign countries have been treated at their facility in Memphis, Tennessee.

St. Jude's Hospital is one of the leading research and treatment facilities for children with cancer and other catastrophic diseases. This hospital is America's second-largest health-care charity. No patient is turn away due to their inability to pay for services.

Their dedication to science and research is well-known across the globe. They continually search for new treatment and cures so that children do not have to suffer.

Visit www.stjude.org to learn more about this hospital as well as ways that you can support their efforts.

Appreciate the medical facilities, health care options, and numerous medical personnel available to us today.

* *Assignment Whisper* *

October 10

Volunteer at your local historical society today.

You will be amazed at the variety of events hosted by the historical society. They regularly have speakers and host fundraisers that are not just about history.

Some ideas to support this group include:

❖ Providing clerical support.
❖ Advertising events.
❖ Organizing library collections.
❖ Assisting others with family research.
❖ Hosting a fundraiser.
❖ Assisting with lecture series.
❖ Contributing articles and photos of your own family history.
❖ Photographing cemeteries for researchers.
❖ Preparing virtual exhibits.
❖ Setting up or removing exhibits.
❖ Developing and maintaining websites.

Finding your local historical society is as easy as conducting an internet search or contacting your local library.

Appreciate the history of your family and your geographic location today. Teach your children about your family's history and the history of the area where you are currently living.

October 11

Volunteer at any small business that only has a handful of employees today.

You may know someone who owns their own business or works for a small company. New businesses and start-up companies can use extra hands and teachable spirits. Depending on the situation, you might be able to take your children with you, too.

Donate your time to helping this small business get a good footing in the community. Do those tasks that take time that no one else has. Answer the phone. Run errands. Be a delivery person. Man the copy machine. Greet customers. Fill orders. Dust shelves. Whatever the need is to help the business thrive, be willing to do it for a day.

Appreciate the entrepreneurial spirit of the business owners today. Let them know how much you appreciate their contribution to the community.

October 12

Appreciate wedding planners today.

Volunteer to provide child care at someone's wedding or wedding rehearsal. If you do not know anyone planning a wedding, ask your church secretary or wedding planner for information.

Weddings and other family events can be challenging for families with small children. They may not be able to include the children in the festivities. If their regular babysitters are family members, they are not available as the entire family is attending the event, too. What's a mother to do?

That is where you step in. Most churches have child care rooms. You can stay there with the children, close to their parents. If the children are similar in age to your children, you may be more comfortable bringing the children to your home. Remember that if you do not know the bride and groom, they might not agree to that arrangement.

Appreciate the predicament of wedding planners today and volunteer to help.

October 13

<u>What My Mother Taught Me</u>
Author Unknown

1. My mother taught me to appreciate a job well done. "If you're going to kill each other, do it outside. I just finished cleaning."
2. My mother taught me religion. "You better pray that will come out of the carpet."
3. My mother taught me about time travel. "If you don't straighten up, I'm going to knock you into the middle of next week!"
4. My mother taught me logic. "Because I said so, that's why."
5. My mother taught me more logic. "If you fall out of that swing and break your neck, you're not going to the store with me."
6. My mother taught me foresight. "Make sure you wear clean underwear, in case you're in an accident."
7. My mother taught me irony. "Keep crying, and I'll give you something to cry about."
8. My mother taught me about the science of osmosis. "Shut your mouth and eat your supper."
9. My mother taught me about contortionism. "Will you look at that dirt on the back of your neck!"
10. My mother taught me about stamina. "You'll sit there until all that spinach is gone."
11. My mother taught me about weather. "This room of yours looks as if a tornado went through it."
12. My mother taught me about hypocrisy. "If I told you once, I've told you a million times. Don't exaggerate!"
13. My mother taught me the circle of life. "I brought you into this world, and I can take you out."

14. My mother taught me about behavior modification. "Stop acting like your father!"
15. My mother taught me about envy. "There are millions of less fortunate children in this world who don't have wonderful parents like you do."
16. My mother taught me about anticipation. "Just wait until we get home."
17. My mother taught me about receiving. "You are going to get it when you get home!"
18. My mother taught me medical science. "If you don't stop crossing your eyes, they're going to freeze that way."
19. My mother taught me ESP. "Put your sweater on; don't you think I know when you are cold?"
20. My mother taught me humor. "When that lawn mower cuts off your toes, don't come running to me."
21. My mother taught me how to become an adult. "If you don't eat your vegetables, you'll never grow up."
22. My mother taught me genetics. "You're just like your father."
23. My mother taught me about my roots. "Shut that door behind you. Do you think you were born in a barn?"
24. My mother taught me wisdom. "When you get to be my age, you'll understand."
25. My mother taught me justice. "One day you'll have kids, and I hope they turn out just like you!"

What will your children remember that you taught them? Are you modeling the behavior that you want them to learn? What do you need to change?

Appreciate what your parents taught you today. Their lessons shaped who you are.

October 14

Appreciate literacy today.

Donate children's books to a local hospital, Ronald McDonald House, Fisher House, United Through Reading, etc.

If you have children, select a few books that they have outgrown. Ask them to help with the selection so that they appreciate where the books are going and who the books will benefit.

If you do not have children, investigate when your library will be having their next book sale. You can also find bargain books at discount book stores. Ask your neighbors with children to contribute, or purchase new books to donate.

Children love variety as much as adults. If adults appreciate a variety of reading sources while waiting in public places, then kids will be grateful for them, too. Parents will benefit from their children being entertained as well.

Encourage literacy today.

* *Assignment Whisper* *

October 15

Pray for a missing child today.

No parent wants to consider the thought of their child being abducted. However, the sad fact remains that it happens far more often than anyone wants to discuss.

The United States Department of Justice reports:

- ❖ 797,500 children (younger than 18) were reported missing in a one-year period of time studied resulting in an average of 2,185 children being reported missing each day.
- ❖ 203,900 children were the victims of family abductions.
- ❖ 58,200 children were the victims of non-family abductions.
- ❖ 115 children were victims of "stereotypical" kidnapping.

For information on how you can help children in need, visit one of these websites:

❖www.missingkids.com
❖www.klaaskids.org/index.htm
❖www.amw.com/missing_children
❖www.childsearch.org
❖www.missingchildren.com

October 16

Distribute identification kits to the neighborhood children today.

After learning the statistics of child abduction yesterday, it is important to protect our children. Contact your local police station to schedule a McGruff event in your neighborhood. Visit www.mcgruff-safe-kids.com to learn more.

Other organizations that promote the protection of our children include these:

❖ www.yoursafechild.com
❖ www.childidprogram.com
❖ www.pollyklaasaction.org
❖ www.ezchildid.com
❖ www.amberalert.com/id-kit.php

Become actively involved in protecting the children in your community. Provide a foundation of safety in which they can grow and prosper. Confident children produce competent adults, the groundwork of our future.

* *Assignment Whisper* *

October 17

Appreciate the lawyers in the world today.

Most of us hope to get through life without ever needing a lawyer. We associate lawyers with lawsuits, traffic tickets, accidents, death, and wills. None of these are pleasant thoughts.

Lawyers actually do perform a valuable service to the community as well as to individuals. Their services can protect people and eliminate problems before they occur. The documents they can execute on your behalf protect your loved ones in the event of your death or physical harm that prevents you from working, for example.

While lawyers as a profession are the brunt of many cruel and sad jokes, they are individuals and real people, too. Large numbers of lawyers chose their profession to help people, not be the source of pain.

Encourage a lawyer today. Show appreciation for his or her contribution to your community.

October 18

<u>That is Enough</u>
Author Unknown

A sick man turned to his doctor, as he was preparing to leave the examination room and said, "Doctor, I am afraid to die. Tell me what lies on the other side."

Very quietly, the doctor said, "I don't know."

"You don't know? You, a Christian man, do not know what is on the other side?"

The doctor was holding the handle of the door; on the other side of which came a sound of scratching and whining, and as he opened the door, a dog sprang into the room and leaped on him with an eager show of gladness.

Turning to the patient, the doctor said, "Did you notice my dog? He's never been in this room before. He didn't know what was inside. He knew nothing except that his master was here, and when the door opened, he sprang in without fear. I know little of what is on the other side of death, but I do know one thing...I know my Master is there and that is enough."

Are you afraid of what is on the other side of a major decision in your life? Invite God into your decision, and your fear will vanish.

* *Assignment Whisper* *

October 19

Thank the telephone operator today.

The operator services are largely performed by technology today. It is rare that dialing "zero" actually connects you with a live person. However, a real person is still on the receiving end of your call. If the automated options cannot answer your question, a real person will come on the line to assist you.

Dial "zero" on your telephone today and connect with a live person. Once you hear his or her voice, express your appreciation that there are still real people answering the phone. Let the operator know how much you appreciate the fact that not everything is done by a machine. Tell them that you realize their job is important, even though your contact with them is so brief.

Imagine a world without telephones or telephone operators. Appreciate the communication they facilitate in our everyday lives.

* Assignment Whisper *

October 20

Donate a ream of paper to the local library's copy room today.

Libraries are funded with county tax dollars. Everything they have is dependent on county budgets being able to accommodate them. Since tax dollars only stretch so far, libraries often receive the first cuts when budgets need adjusting.

Any donation that you are able to make to your local library benefits the entire community. If you are thinking to yourself that you cannot remember the last time you used your local library, it is time to go. You will be amazed at the volume of people that pass through their doors each day. People of all ages and walks of life use the library for a variety of reasons. Mothers take their children for after school programs. Adults use the computers for job searches. Teens use the library for researching school papers. All ages use it as a source of information on any number of topics.

Reacquaint yourself with the local library today. Take a package of paper with you. The librarian may be amused at your donation, but she will be appreciative at the same time.

* *Assignment Whisper* *

October 21

Plant flowers around a historical marker today.

In some parts of the country, this may not be a practical time of year to do this. If flowers will not grow this time of year, clean up the area. Rake the leaves. Remove the trash. Give the area around the marker a face lift.

If you are able to plant flowers, plant something native to the area. Research into the topic of the sign and investigate what native plant would best complement the subject matter of the marker. Make the area attractive for those who stop to read it.

Visit www.hmdb.org to locate the markers nearest to you.

If there are no markers convenient to your home, create your own historical marker in your yard. Document a significant event in your family's life, and create a memorial to that happy occasion. Keep your family's history alive for the next generation.

* *Assignment Whisper* *

October 22

<u>Book recommendation</u>
Do Hard Things by Alex and Brett Harris is a must read for all ages.

Alex and Brett are twin teenaged brothers who wrote this book in August 2005. Since that time, their "rebelution" has grown beyond anything they imagined. Their book is written by teens, about teens, and for teens. The brothers challenge their audience to do things considered beyond the abilities of teenagers by most of society. It encourages parents to push their children to be the best that they can be.

For me personally, *Do Hard Things* was one of the motivating forces behind this devotional. As I read, it occurred to me that their ideas could be applied to adults as well. So often in my life, I have met tired and apathetic women who become so wrapped up in their daily grind that they cannot see the possibilities of their lives. I talk to husbands who are on automatic with their careers and miss creating a life with their families. The change is so gradual that people fall in the pit before they even see the hole in the ground.

My hope is that this devotional will motivate and inspire men and women of all ages to climb out of the pit and rise to new levels. Challenge yourself to see what you could be instead of only what you are today. Be inspired to do more and be present to the people in your life.

Read the book by the Harris brothers and make a plan to do hard things regardless of your age.

* *Assignment Whisper* *

October 23

If you are still looking for ideas to inspire you, visit one of these websites for more opportunities:
- ❖ www.usafreedomcorps.gov
- ❖ www.citizencorps.gov

These two websites contain many ideas and information on volunteer programs that might interest you.

If you are at this point in the devotional and still feel that you have not found your passion, do not despair. The goal is to whisper to others, not build yourself up. You may not have witnessed the impact of your actions throughout the year, but rest assured that you have made a difference in your world.

The Bible often teaches lessons on discipleship in farming terms. You will notice, however, that the parables discuss the sowing, not the harvesting, of the seeds. Man does the sowing, but the harvest belongs to God alone.

Read the Parable of the Sower in Matthew 13 and notice that there is no mention of the harvest. Again in I Corinthians 15:37 we are reminded that we plant the seed and not the body that it will be.

When you sow, you do not plant the body that will be, but just a seed, perhaps of wheat or of something else.

Do not worry about the seeds you have sown while whispering. God will harvest your seeds in His own time. Continue to sow in order that God's harvest may be bountiful and fruitful.

* *Assignment Whisper* *

October 24

Consider volunteering for the Peace Corp.

Peace Corps Volunteers work in the following areas: education, youth outreach, and community development; business development; agriculture and environment; health and HIV/AIDS; and information technology. Within these areas, the specific duties and responsibilities of each Volunteer can vary widely. Their website is:
www.peacecorps.gov.

For most of us, this is a radical idea. Relocating to another country, working in impoverished areas of the world, and risking our own personal health and safety to serve others does not sound like something that appeals to the average person. I still encourage you to spend some time on their website gathering more information. You might be amazed at the opportunities that exist from the comfort of your own home.

* *Assignment Whisper* *

October 25

Is it a bird? A plane? Could it be........? You do not need to be Superman to impact flying. Yes, the red cape would be fun, but you can soar without one on today's whispering assignment.

Contact your local airport chaplain to volunteer at the chapel. Most large airports have clergy on staff for travelers in need of counseling or encouraging. Chapels provide a quiet retreat for passengers who wish to spend their lay-over time in prayer. Smaller airports might surprise you with regard to the spiritual services offered.

Some supportive ideas for airport chapels include:
❖Donate flowers for the altar.
❖Provide Bibles.
❖Contribute candles if they are allowed.
❖Offer instrumental music discs.
❖Conduct a Bible study or prayer group.
❖Supply facial tissues.
❖Treat the chaplain to lunch.
❖Note your ideas here.

Contact the airport's chaplain before your arrival. Ask for suggestions and guidelines for volunteers. Remember to ask if the red cape is optional or required.

* *Assignment Whisper* *

October 26

Volunteer with an adult literacy program today.

According to the National Assessment of Adult Literacy, there was no significant increase in adult literacy scores between 1992 and 2003. The adult illiteracy rate in the United States is approximately 38% and stable. More than one third of the people in any given group cannot read. Think of that the next time you are at the movie theater or grocery store.

Volunteering with adult literacy does not require a teaching degree or professional experience. All you need to know is how to read and have patience. Adults are more likely to be ashamed of their lack of reading skills than children. Your smile and encouraging words creating a relaxed atmosphere that boosts self-confidence and encourages learning.

This website will help you to get started: www.proliteracy.org/NetCommunity.

You can also contact your local library or community center for more information.

* *Assignment Whisper* *

October 27

Volunteer for your community's CERT program.

The Community Emergency Response Team (CERT) program helps train people to be better prepared to respond to emergency situations in their communities. When emergencies happen, CERT members can give critical support to first responders, provide immediate assistance to victims, and organize spontaneous volunteers at a disaster site. CERT members can also help with non-emergency projects that help improve the safety of the community.

The CERT course is taught in the community by a trained team of first responders who have completed a CERT Train-the-Trainer course conducted by their state training office for emergency management, or FEMA's Emergency Management Institute (EMI). CERT training includes disaster preparedness, disaster fire suppression, basic disaster medical operations, and light search and rescue operations.

Natural disasters happen in all areas of our nation. The Gulf Coast has hurricanes. California has wild fires. The Midwest has tornadoes and floods. The Northeast has blizzards. Be prepared to assist your community when the need arises.

Visit www.citizencorps.gov/cert/about.shtm for the source of this information as well as ways to become involved in your community.

October 28

Volunteer with Points of Light organizations in your community today.

Points of Light Institute's website describes the three main goals as follows:

❖Citizen Action: Create an engaged citizenry where every individual has the opportunity to make a difference through meaningful civic engagement.

❖Civic Infrastructure: Develop a civic infrastructure equipped with the resources, tools, and knowledge to create change in communities.

❖Campaigns for Impact: Demonstrate the power of citizens actively engaged in changing our world and solving problems.

The opportunities vary from city to city. If you have a particular skill or resource that is not currently being utilized in your area, consider organizing this for your community.

Visit www.pointsoflight.org to get started.

* *Assignment Whisper* *

October 29

Volunteer with Tech Corps today.

While visiting the website, you will learn:

"Tech Corps is the leading national non-profit mobilizing technology volunteers into schools, offering tech support and teacher training. They offer high quality technological resources that enrich K-12 teaching and learning and prepare tomorrow's workforce.

Tech Corps was founded in 1995 by Gary J. Beach, Publisher of CIO Magazine. Beach envisioned an organization which would challenge millions of American volunteers to build a technology infrastructure much like the Peace Corps challenges men and women to help build infrastructure in developing countries. In a recent year, Tech Corps state chapters deployed some 6,000 volunteers into 1,500 schools nationally, accumulating nearly 100,000 volunteer hours, providing roughly $5 million of tech support and teacher training."

Visit their website at http://techcorps.org/ for more information.

October 30

Volunteer with the Juvenile Diabetes Association.

Today approximately 23.6 million people, or 7.8 percent of the population, have diabetes. The estimated direct cost of diabetes in America in 2007 was $116 billion. The indirect cost (disability, work loss, premature mortality) was estimated to be $58 billion. These numbers do not take into account the emotional cost of having a child with juvenile diabetes.

Juvenile diabetes is the focus of today because of Halloween tomorrow. Regardless of your opinion of Halloween, imagine being a mother of a child with diabetes and telling them they cannot participate because of their illness. What would it be like to explain to your child that a day that most kids enjoy and anticipate could damage their health?

Volunteer to help those struggling with a disease that has no cure. Offer to host an alternative to Halloween party for kids who want the fellowship and fun without the risk of death.

For more information, visit:

❖www.jdrf.org

❖http://diabetes.niddk.nih.gov

* *Assignment Whisper* *

October 31

Happy Halloween! Since I write this devotional from an unapologetic Christian perspective, that statement may seem inappropriate to you. However, I say it anyway. This is why.

October 31 is just a day like any other day. Some aspects of the festivities and history of Halloween are very offensive to me. However, when it is all said and done, it is still just a day. Candy is just candy.

The thing about Halloween that bothers me the most is that it causes such tension and division among people. Between "good Christian people" the question of trick-or-treating can ruin friendships and consume church councils for weeks. When you add non-Christians to the conversation, the debate gets far more heated. What does this accomplish?

God did not want a spirit of strife and discontent between His people. God's vision is for His people to be one family on earth. Jesus instructs us to love one another and serve our neighbor. I believe that God would have encouraged us to love the neighbor who knocks on our door wearing a costume as well.

This Halloween, try to find the humor in the situation. When you find yourself disagreeing with others about their views on Halloween, pray to God to enlighten your heart on *His* view on the subject. Show love and unity to those who disagree with you. Find another subject that will build your relationship instead of constructing walls between you.

I am not suggesting that you change your ideas about Halloween based on what others do. Prayerfully listen to God on the subject, and refrain from allowing one day of the year to tear down people and relationships.

* *Assignment Whisper* *

November 1

November is the month when people think about Thanksgiving. That means food. It also means taking inventory of our many blessings.

Spend some time today thanking God for His abundance and provisions in your life. The fact that you can read this devotional is a blessing in itself. Say thank you for your eyesight, Gutenberg for inventing the printing press, and the fact that you can afford to purchase books. That is just the start of the list.

Before the holidays arrive, remember God's generosity in your life.

For if, by the trespass of the one man [Adam], death reigned through that one man, how much more will those who receive God's abundant provision of grace and of the gift of righteousness reign in life through the one man, Jesus Christ.
Romans 5:17

Ask and it will be given to you; seek and you will find; knock and the door will be opened to you.
Matthew 7:7

November 2

Thank your spouse for working to support the family today.

If your spouse works outside of the home, thank them for providing financially as well as emotionally to your family. If you have children, the work does not end when you come home. In effect, you have two jobs. Thank your spouse for doing both.

If your spouse does not work outside of the home, thank your spouse for being the CEO of your household. Thank them for doing the tasks necessary to keep a household operational.

While cash is important, it takes more than financial support to keep a home and a family running smoothly. Appreciate all of the things that your spouse does to make this happen for all of you.

If you feel that your spouse is a lazy bum who contributes nothing, think again. If you really put some thought into it, chances are high that you will be able to find something that your spouse contributes. Give them a chance to prove you wrong about the lazy bum part!

* *Assignment Whisper* *

November 3

Thank your children for helping around the house today. Show them how thankful you are that they contribute to the household.

I read an article once about motivating your children to help around the house. The idea was to put everything that your children left laying around the house in a box. The only way that they could retrieve their things from the box was to do an extra chore around the house. For example, if your child left their favorite game on the floor, mom put it in the box until they cleaned the bathroom or took out the trash. With this system in place, the chore most often picked by the children was to clean up after their siblings. By putting their siblings' discarded belongings in the box, their siblings had to do the nastiest chores to retrieve them. I like this idea!

It is not effective in our home, however, because we have only one child. The sibling rivalry is just not a motivating force. The technique we use instead is of one of appreciation. We taught our daughter that household chores are fun to do together and simply something that life requires.

Whether you have chores or clean up "games" in your home, being appreciated is still something that everyone craves. Tell your children thank you today in a special way. Print some homemade certificates. Take them out for ice cream. Rent a fun movie. Plan a trip to the park for the weekend. Your kids will be far more motivated to help with chores when they know they are appreciated.

Assignment Whisper

November 4

"Joy increases as you give it,
and diminishes as you try to keep it for yourself.
In giving it, you will accumulate a deposit of joy
greater than you ever believed possible."
Norman Vincent Peale

I sincerely hope that by this time in the year you have found joy in whispering to others. I pray that this joy has increased not only your own personal satisfaction with life but has also increased the time that you have to appreciate that joy. I have found that the more time I spend serving others, the more time I have to do additional things. Putting others first is the only effective means of adding hours to your days. Do something for someone today that makes them joyful. This might be as simple as smiling at them. It might be something that takes the majority of the day. It might require you to sweat and do manual labor, or it might mean cuddling on the sofa with a good book and a gaggle of children around you.

Increase the joy today. Accumulate your deposit of joy in the process.

November 5

In the New Testament, "thankfulness" means:
1) grace
   a) that which affords joy, pleasure, delight, sweetness, charm, loveliness: grace of speech
2) good will, loving-kindness, favor
   a) of the merciful kindness by which God, exerting his holy influence upon souls, turns them to Christ, keeps, strengthens, increases them in Christian faith, knowledge, affection, and kindles them to the exercise of the Christian virtues
3) what is due to grace
   a) the spiritual condition of one governed by the power of divine grace
   b) the token or proof of grace, benefit
      1) a gift of grace
      2) benefit, bounty
4) thanks, (for benefits, services, favors), reward, recompense

Webster's definition goes like this:
   1. conscious of benefit received
   2. expressive of thanks
   3. well pleased : glad

How do you define "thankfulness?"

November 6

To put the world right in order,
we must first put the nation in order;
to put the nation in order,
we must first put the family in order;
to put the family in order,
we must first cultivate our personal life;
we must first set our hearts right.

Confucius

Confucius was born in 551 BC and died when he was 72 years old. His words, however, have lived forever. Who among us can say that they have never heard Confucius quoted?

While his words are 2,500 years old, the meaning still holds true today. We must first set our own hearts right before tackling the world. Perhaps you have noticed a pattern in this devotional. The first day of the month is about God. The second day focused on your spouse, and the third day of each month was reserved for your children. Take care of your own house first before branching out into the community and nation.

Have you been whispering to yourself and your family effectively this year? Are there still areas that need work before your joy is complete at home? Take inventory before the end of the year. Plan now to start the new year with the joy in your own heart on solid ground.

November 7

Participate in a walk or run for a cause today.

There are many organizations that do these events throughout the year. Depending on where you live, this might be the height of the season.

If you have never done this before, try it once. You will find that they are more fun and there is more camaraderie than you imagine. Most runs encourage walkers as well. You can also find events that support strollers and families participating together.

St. Jude's Hospital hosts their annual run in early December.

The Breast Cancer foundation has their annual 3-day event in several cities in November. Visit www.the3day.org to find the locations and dates.

The Arthritis Foundation has an event called Joints in Motion. www.arthritis.org/run-walk.php

Team Parkinson is ready to get you into shape for their next event at www.team-parkinson.org.

If you are not a runner, consider hosting an event in your area. These websites will help get you started:

- ❖ http://stepbystepfundraising.com/marathon-training-program/
- ❖ http://www.marathonrookie.com/marathon-for-charity.html

* *Assignment Whisper* *

November 8

There was a little old lady who was very spiritual who would step out on her porch every day, raise her arms to the sky and yell "Praise the Lord."

One day, an atheist bought the house next door to her, and he became very irritated with the spiritual lady. So after a month or so of her yelling, "Praise the Lord" from her porch, he went outside on his porch and yelled back, "There is no Lord."

Yet, the little old lady continued.

One cold, wintry day, when the little old lady couldn't get to the store, she went out on her porch, raised her hands up to the sky and said, "Help me Lord, I have no more money, it's cold, and I have no more food."

The next morning, she went outside, and there were three bags of food on the porch, enough to last her a week. "Praise the Lord," she yelled.

The Atheist stepped out from the bushes and said, "There is no Lord hahaha, I bought those groceries!"

The little old lady raised her arms to the sky and said, "Praise the Lord, you sent me groceries and you made the Devil pay for them."

Be thankful for the difficult people in your life. God put them there for a reason.

* *Assignment Whisper* *

November 9

Volunteer with Junior Achievement today.

Their website highlights these facts about this worthy organization:

"Junior Achievement Worldwide is the world's largest organization dedicated to educating students about workforce readiness, entrepreneurship, and financial literacy through experiential, hands-on programs.

Junior Achievement programs help prepare young people for the real world by showing them how to generate wealth and effectively manage it, how to create jobs which make their communities more robust, and how to apply entrepreneurial thinking to the workplace. Students put these lessons into action and learn the value of contributing to their communities.

JA's unique approach allows volunteers from the community to deliver our curriculum while sharing their experiences with students. Embodying the heart of JA, our 287,000 classroom volunteers transform the key concepts of our lessons into a message that inspires and empowers students to believe in themselves, showing them they can make a difference in the world."

Visit www.ja.org to discover how your talents align with Junior Achievement.

November 10

Here's a little mathematical formula that might inspire you. The author is unknown to me.

If: A B C D E F G H I J K L M N O P Q R S T U V W X Y Z
Is represented as: 1 2 3 4 5 6 7 8 9 10 11 12 13 14 15 16 17 18 19 20 21 22 23 24 25 26.

Then: H-A-R-D-W-O-R- K
8+1+18+4+23+15+18+11 = 98%

And: K-N-O-W-L-E-D-G-E
11+14+15+23+12+5+4+7+5 = 96%

But: A-T-T-I-T-U-D-E
1+20+20+9+20+21+4+5 = 100%

THEN, look how far the love of God will take you:
L-O-V-E-O-F-G-O-D
12+15+22+5+15+6+7+15+4 = 101%

Therefore, one can conclude with mathematical certainty that: While Hard Work and Knowledge will get you close, and Attitude will get you there, It's the Love of God that will put you over the top!

November 11

Organize a toy drive and donate the gifts to Toys for Tots.

Each year the Toys for Tots program, sponsored by the United States Marine Reserves, distributes gifts to needy children in the community for Christmas. The organization's stated mission is as follows:

"The primary goal of Toys for Tots is to deliver, through a shiny new toy at Christmas, a message of hope to needy youngsters that will motivate them to grow into responsible, productive, patriotic citizens and community leaders."

The Toys for Tots Literacy Program specifically collects books to distribute to the children. Literacy will improve a child's chances of becoming productive members of the community, improve their self-esteem, and encourage them to achieve their goals.

Visit www.toysfortots.org for more information.

Plan now to host a party and ask your friends to bring a toy to donate to this worthy cause. This party can be for all ages and stages of life.

November 12

Consider hosting a foreign exchange student.

If this is not something that you feel you and your family can do, find a host family and volunteer to entertain their student for a day or a weekend for them.

While having a foreign exchange student in your home can be a fabulous experience, it still means that the host family has no time alone while the student is there. Invite the student to spend an evening with your family to give the host family some time alone.

If you do not know of agencies that serve your area, contact your local public high school for information on host families. Some other agencies to explore are:

❖www.ayusa.org

❖www.asse.com

❖www.foreignexchangestudent.com

* *Assignment Whisper* *

November 13

If you are considering a new hair style for the new year, donate your hair to Locks of Love.

Locks of Love is an organization that provides hairpieces to financially disadvantaged children under age 18 who are suffering from long-term medical hair loss from any diagnosis. Their mission is to, "return a sense of self, confidence and normalcy to children suffering from hair loss by utilizing donated ponytails to provide the highest quality hair prosthetics to financially disadvantaged children."

Donating hair might be a stretch for some of you as they require a minimum of ten inches for a donation. If you do not have ten inches of hair to spare, there are other ways that you can help this praiseworthy association. If you own a hair salon or work at one, encourage the stylists at the salon to become a Participating Salon. The next time you get your own hair cut, talk to your stylist about promoting this in their business.

Visit www.locksoflove.org for more information.

* *Assignment Whisper* *

November 14

Volunteer to deliver Meals on Wheels for the holidays. This idea has been mentioned before in this devotional. If you are still involved in this ministry, bless you! If you never tried it before, please do so now for the holiday season.

Meals on Wheels' website www.mowaa.org will provide you with more information regarding the events planned in your area for the next two months. The time commitment that they ask of their volunteers is minimal. In as little as two hours a month, you can significantly impact someone's world and ensure that they do not go to bed with an empty stomach.

Meals on Wheels is also a project that the entire family can do. Get the kids to make cards or draw pictures. If you have aspiring movie producers in your house, have them record a short movie to share. Practice Christmas carols to sing with the people you visit. Everyone will have a good time.

November 15

Consider teaching a class at the local community center or library.

Whatever your skill may be, plan now to share in the coming year. Librarians are planning their January calendars now. Community Centers are printing advertising flyers. YMCA's are prompting parents to bring their children to more classes after the holidays. Get your name and class on their lists.

Remember that the goal of most classes like this is not to make professionals out of their students. Most of these classes focus on education and entertainment. Beginner classes in a wide variety of subjects are encouraged and enjoyed by all ages. You could teach knitting, cake decorating, scrapbooking, whittling, or yoga. Whatever skill you have is worth sharing.

November 16

<u>Perspective: The Invisible Woman</u>
By Nicole Johnson

It started to happen gradually. One day, I was walking my son Jake to school. I was holding his hand, and we were about to cross the street when the crossing guard said to him, "Who is that with you, young fella?"

"Nobody," he shrugged.

"Nobody?" said the crossing guard, and I laughed. My son is only 5, but as we crossed the street I thought, "Oh my goodness, nobody?"

I would walk into a room, and no one would notice. I would say something to my family like, "Turn the TV down, please," - and nothing would happen. Nobody would get up, or even make a move for the remote. I would stand there for a minute, and then I would say again, a little louder, "Would someone turn the TV down?" Nothing.

Just the other night, my husband and I were out at a party. We'd been there for about three hours, and I was ready to leave. I noticed he was talking to a friend from work. So I walked over, and when there was a break in the conversation, I whispered, "I'm ready to go when you are." He just kept right on talking.

That's when I started to put all the pieces together. I don't think he can see me. I don't think anyone can see me. I'm invisible.

It all began to make sense, the blank stares, the lack of response, the way one of the kids will walk into the room while I'm on the phone and ask to be taken to the store. Inside I'm thinking, "Can't you see I'm on the phone?"

Obviously not! No one can see if I'm on the phone, or cooking, or sweeping the floor, or even standing on my head in the corner, because no one can see me at all.

I'm invisible.

Some days, I am only a pair of hands, nothing more: Can you fix this? Can you tie this? Can you open this? Some days I'm not a pair of hands; I'm not even a human being. I'm a clock to ask, "What time is it?" I'm a satellite guide to answer, "What number is the Disney Channel?" I'm a car to order, "Right around 5:30, please."

I was certain that these were the hands that once held books and the eyes that studied history and the mind that graduated summa cum laude -but now they had disappeared into the peanut butter, never to be seen again.

She's going-- she's going-- she's gone!

One night, a group of us were having dinner, celebrating the return of a friend from England. Janice had just gotten back from a fabulous trip, and she was going on and on about the hotel she stayed in. I was sitting there, looking around at the others all put together so well. It was hard not to compare and feel sorry for myself as I looked down at my out-of-style dress; it was the only thing I could find that was clean. My unwashed hair was pulled up in a banana clip, and I was afraid I could actually smell peanut butter in it. I was feeling pretty pathetic, when Janice turned to me with a beautifully wrapped package, and said, "I brought you this."

It was a book on the great cathedrals of Europe. I wasn't exactly sure why she'd given it to me until I read her inscription: "To Charlotte, with admiration for the greatness of what you are building when no one sees."

In the days ahead I would read - no, devour - the book. And I would discover what would become for me, four life-changing truths, after which I could pattern my work:

    * No one can say who built the great cathedrals - we have no record of their names.

    * These builders gave their whole lives for a work they would never see finished.

    * They made great sacrifices and expected no credit.

    * The passion of their building was fueled by their faith that the eyes of God saw everything.

A legendary story in the book told of a rich man who came to visit the cathedral while it was being built, and he saw a workman carving a tiny bird on the inside of a beam! He was puzzled and asked the man, "Why are you spending so much time carving that bird into a beam that will be covered by the roof? No one will ever see it."

And the workman replied, "Because God sees."

I closed the book, feeling the missing piece fall into place. It was almost as if I heard God whispering to me, "I see you, Charlotte. I see the sacrifices you make every day, even when no one around you does. No act of kindness you've done, no sequin you've sewn on, no cupcake you've baked, is too small for me to notice and smile over. You are building a great cathedral, but you can't see right now what it will become."

At times, my invisibility feels like an affliction. But it is not a disease that is erasing my life. It is the cure for the disease of my own self-centeredness. It is the antidote to my strong, stubborn pride.

I keep the right perspective when I see myself as a great builder. As one of the people who show up at a job that they will never see finished, to work on something that their name will never be on. The writer of the book went so far as to say that no cathedrals could ever be built in our lifetime because there are so few people willing to sacrifice to that degree.

When I really think about it, I don't want my son to tell the friend he's bringing home from college for Thanksgiving, "My mom gets up at 4 in the morning and bakes homemade pies, and then she hand bastes a turkey for three hours and presses all the linens for the table." That would mean I'd built a shrine or a monument to myself. I just want him to want to come home. And then, if there is anything more to say to his friend, to add, "You're gonna love it there."

As mothers, we are building great cathedrals. We cannot be seen if we're doing it right. And one day, it is very possible that the world will marvel, not only at what we have built, but at the beauty that has been added to the world by the sacrifices of invisible women.

November 17

Make a "thankful" calendar for yourself and your family. Each day, note one thing that you are thankful for, who gave it to you, and where you received it.

You can make separate calendars for each of your family members, or you could make one calendar to complete together. Post it on your refrigerator or someplace central to your family's gatherings. Set aside a specific time each day for your family to add to the list.

Save this calendar for your children's' baby books. When they are older, this will be a fun walk down memory lane for them.

Use this calendar to create a thankful character in your household as well as each individual family member. Young children need to start this habit now. Older kids really can be taught new tricks.

"You cannot dream yourself into a character; you must hammer and forge yourself one."

Henry David Thoreau

* *Assignment Whisper* *

November 18

One afternoon a man came home from work to find total mayhem in his house. His three children were outside, still in their pajamas, playing in the mud, with empty food boxes and wrappers strewn all around the front yard. The door of his wife's car was open, as was the front door to the house and there was no sign of the dog.

Proceeding into the entry, he found an even bigger mess. A lamp had been knocked over, and the throw rug was wadded against one wall. In the front room the TV was loudly blaring a cartoon channel, and the family room was strewn with toys and various items of clothing. In the kitchen, dishes filled the sink, breakfast food was spilled on the counter, the fridge door was open wide, dog food was spilled on the floor, a broken glass lay under the table, and a small pile of sand was spread by the back door.

He quickly headed up the stairs, stepping over toys and more piles of clothes, looking for his wife. He was worried she may be ill, or that something serious had happened. He was met with a small trickle of water as it made its way out the bathroom door. As he peered inside he found wet towels, scummy soap and more toys strewn over the floor. Miles of toilet paper lay in a heap and toothpaste had been smeared over the mirror and walls. As he rushed to the bedroom, he found his wife still curled up in the bed in her pajamas, reading a novel. She looked up at him, smiled, and asked how his day went.

He looked at her bewildered and asked, "What happened here today?"

She again smiled and answered, "You know every day when you come home from work and you ask me what in the world did I do today?"

"Yes" was his incredulous reply.

The answered, "Well, today I didn't do it."

Appreciate your spouse today. Verbalize your knowledge of what he or she contributes to the family. Imagine what you would learn if you switched places with your spouse for one day!

.

* *Assignment Whisper* *

November 19

<u>Book recommendation</u>
Practicing in the Presence of People: How we learn to Love by Mike Mason is an astonishing book.

If you remember, I recommended another one of Mr. Mason's books last April. All of his books have been thought-provoking and inspirational in my life. He challenges me to see things from a unique perspective. I encourage you to read this book and learn from it. The summary of this book reads:

"In the deepest part of our hearts and souls is the desire to love well. Yet in our struggle to do so, we learn that, as Mike Mason puts it, "We are not born with love; it is something we must learn." Now, in *Practicing the Presence of People,* he helps us launch that learning process. Mason points the way to fresh knowledge and fresh experience, showing how we can discover new things about those we love, understand them from the inside out, tenderly identify with their weaknesses, and celebrate that they too were lovingly made by the hand of God. "

Assignment Whisper

November 20

Give blank thank you notes to your friends and encourage them to write a thank you note to someone in their life today.

As you learn to be thankful this month, it can be frustrating when those around us are not as grateful as they could be. Encourage others today to see their blessings and express appreciation for the gifts they have received. When the lack of appreciation aggravates you, pull a blank card from your purse or briefcase.

Writing thank you notes is a dying habit. Twenty years ago, cards of gratitude followed gifts like ducklings track their mother. Encourage your friends to revive this lost art. Make a game of creating moving sentences and verses. Who knows? You may receive a thank you note for "note writing instruction."

* *Assignment Whisper* *

November 21

A few years ago, at the Seattle Special Olympics, nine contestants, all physically or mentally disabled, assembled at the starting line for the 100-yard dash. At the gun, they all started out, not exactly in a dash, but with a relish to run the race to the finish and win. All, that is, except one little boy who stumbled on the asphalt, tumbled over a couple of times, and began to cry. The other eight heard the boy cry. They slowed down and looked back. Then they all turned around and went back......every one of them.

One girl with Down's Syndrome bent down and kissed him and said, "This will make it better."

Then all nine linked arms and walked together to the finish line. Everyone in the stadium stood, and the cheering went on for several minutes. People who were there are still telling the story.

Why? Because deep down we know this one thing: What matters in this life is more than winning for ourselves. What matters in this life is helping others win, even if it means slowing down and changing our course.

How do you define "winning?" Are you thankful for the things you have won?

November 22

Are you involved with an organization that is having difficulty recruiting volunteers? Do you find it hard to convince people to whisper with you? Visit Volunteer Solutions for help. Their website is www.volunteersolutions.org.

This site is for both the volunteer as well as the agency needing volunteers. By entering your zip code, you will receive a listing of opportunities in your area.

If you are hosting an event, involved in organizing a fundraiser, or working for a non-profit agency, investigate posting your volunteer needs on this site. Make it easier for potential volunteers to learn of opportunities in their community.

November 23

Donate a turkey to a needy family.

The grocery store where I spend most of my grocery budget gives away free turkeys each year for Thanksgiving. Patrons accumulate points during a specific time period. With enough points, you can earn a free turkey. I make a point to earn a turkey every year and donate it to a family who would otherwise go without one this Thanksgiving.

If your grocery store does not offer programs similar to this, collect the loose change around your house and purchase a turkey to donate. Start a penny jar now to save for next year's turkey donation.

Contact your church or local community center to find a needy family if you do not already know one. Donate it to Meals on Wheels. Offer it to an assisted living center or hospice. Just do not let a free turkey go homeless.

November 24

Do something for the employees at your local oil change shop.

This time of year people are getting their cars tuned up and ready for the road trips to visit family. Repair shops can be swamped with holiday travelers in the weeks before Thanksgiving. Everyone wants to have a trip free of car troubles. The oil change shops are working extra hard this time of year.

Here are some ideas to brighten their day:

- ❖ Take cookies.
- ❖ Write a thank you note. Deliver it in person or put it in the mail.
- ❖ Cut a bouquet of fresh flowers from your garden.
- ❖ Sing a cheerful song with your children.
- ❖ Donate a bottle of degreaser or hand towels.
- ❖ Contribute pens for customers who do not want to use grease-covered pens.
- ❖ Order pizza delivered for lunch.
- ❖ Note your ideas here.

November 25

"A candle loses nothing
by lighting another candle."

I am sorry that I was not able to discover the author of this proverb. I think it is so lovely, simple, and direct.

While whispering this year, how did you feel? Did you feel uplifted and joyful in serving others, or did you feel drained and tired? Did you feel overwhelmed, or did you find that whispering created more time in your life?

If whispering creates a feeling of joy and satisfaction for you, then you must be the flame. If you are left feeling lost and drained, then perhaps you are the wax.

Be thankful that your candles are burning. Strive to light other candles. You will lose nothing.

* *Assignment Whisper* *

November 26

The History of Thanksgiving Day

The Pilgrims set ground at Plymouth Rock on December 11, 1620. Their first winter was devastating. At the beginning of the following fall, they had lost 46 of the original 102 who sailed on the *Mayflower*. But the harvest of 1621 was a bountiful one. And the remaining colonists decided to celebrate with a feast -- including 91 Indians who had helped the Pilgrims survive their first year. It is believed that the Pilgrims would not have made it through the year without the help of the natives. The feast was more of a traditional English harvest festival than a true "thanksgiving" observance. It lasted three days.

This "thanksgiving" feast was not repeated the following year. Many years passed before the event was repeated. It wasn't until June of 1676 that another Day of thanksgiving was proclaimed. On June 20 of that year the governing council of Charlestown, Massachusetts, held a meeting to determine how best to express thanks for the good fortune that had seen their community securely established. By unanimous vote they instructed Edward Rawson, the clerk, to proclaim June 29 as a day of thanksgiving. It is notable that this thanksgiving celebration probably did not include the Indians, as the celebration was meant partly to be in recognition of the colonists' recent victory over the "heathen natives,"

A hundred years later, in October of 1777 all 13 colonies joined in a thanksgiving celebration. It also commemorated the patriotic victory over the British at Saratoga. But it was a one-time affair.

* *Assignment Whisper* *

George Washington proclaimed a National Day of Thanksgiving in 1789, although some were opposed to it. There was discord among the colonies, many feeling the hardships of a few pilgrims did not warrant a national holiday. And later, President Thomas Jefferson opposed the idea of having a day of thanksgiving.

It was Sarah Josepha Hale, a magazine editor, whose efforts eventually led to what we recognize as Thanksgiving. Hale wrote many editorials championing her cause in her *Boston Ladies' Magazine*, and later, in *Godey's Lady's Book*. Finally, after a 40-year campaign of writing editorials and letters to governors and presidents, Hale's obsession became a reality when, in 1863, President Lincoln proclaimed the *last* Thursday in November as a national day of Thanksgiving.

Thanksgiving was proclaimed by every president after Lincoln. The date was changed a couple of times, most recently by Franklin Roosevelt, who set it up one week to the next-to-last Thursday in order to create a longer Christmas shopping season. Public uproar against this decision caused the president to move Thanksgiving back to its original date two years later. And in 1941, Thanksgiving was finally sanctioned by Congress as a legal holiday, as the *fourth* Thursday in November.

(Summarized from
http://wilstar.com/holidays/thankstr.htm)

* *Assignment Whisper* *

November 27

Review the definition of "abundance" today.
Abundance in the New Testament is defined as:
1) to exceed a fixed number of measure, to be left over and above a certain number or measure
   a) to be over, to remain
   b) to exist or be at hand in abundance
      1) to be great (abundant)
      2) a thing which comes in abundance, or overflows unto one, something falls to the lot of one in large measure
      3) to redound unto, turn out abundantly for, a thing
   c) to abound, overflow
      1) to be abundantly furnished with, to have in abundance, to be in affluence, abound in (a thing)
      2) to be pre-eminent, to excel
      3) to excel more than, exceed
2) to make to abound
   a) to furnish one richly so that he has abundance
   b) to make abundant or excellent

Webster's Dictionary defines "abundance" as:
   1. an ample quantity : profusion
   2. affluence, wealth
   3. relative degree of plentifulness

How do you define "abundance" in your life?

* *Assignment Whisper* *

November 28

Volunteer to teach prevention classes for sexually transmitted diseases (STD) in your community.

Sexually transmitted diseases effect people of all ages. While we would like to believe that most people know to be cautious, that is not always the case. Most people operate under the "it would never happen to me" mentality, or once they are exposed, they are embarrassed to seek help and suffer the consequences for many years.

You do not need to have a nursing degree or medical expertise to teach classes. The material can be learned, or you can volunteer to be a teacher's assistant in an existing class.

STDs are robbing our youth of their health at an alarming rate. Adults also suffer the consequences. Abstinence does not always prevent STDs as some can be transmitted through sexual activities that do not involve intercourse.

For more information on how you can help prevent the spread of STDs, contact the Center for Disease Control in your area, or visit their website at: ww.cdcnpin.org. There are outreach materials available online.

* *Assignment Whisper* *

November 29

Clean your closets and donate to the local thrift shop before Christmas.

We all have things in our closets that we do not use. Maybe you have clothes that no longer fit. Perhaps pillows and bedding stuff your closets, or kitchen utensils clogging your drawers. Take some time today to tackle one closet and donate these things to the local thrift shop.

Make shoppers happy this holiday season. Families will soon begin their Christmas shopping. Mothers replenish routine household items. Do your part to ensure that there is something there when they head for the racks this year. If everyone donated one or two items that they no longer use, the thrift stores would be well supplied for those in need.

Besides, it always feels good to have clean closets.

November 30

Gather a couple of shoe boxes and prepare them for donation to the Samaritan's Purse.

From their website:

"Operation Christmas Child brings joy and hope to children in desperate situations around the world through gift-filled shoe boxes and the message of God's unconditional love. Anyone can participate in this simple, hands-on project.

Last season, 661,530 shoe boxes from Canada were collected and distributed to children in more than 15 countries. Each gift is a special reminder to a child that he or she is loved. Delivered by teams of local pastors, charities, and civic leaders, Operation Christmas Child gifts provide opportunities to make a lasting impact on children, families and communities. Often, the shoe boxes open doors to provide other aid, allowing Samaritan's Purse to provide resources for a better tomorrow."

For details regarding how to pack your shoebox and what to include, visit their website at www.samaritanspurse.ca/occ/shoebox.

Give the gift of joy and hope to a child who would otherwise go without any Christmas cheer this year.

December 1

As Christmas approaches, it is appropriate to remember all of the many gifts that God has given us in our lives. Spend some time today thanking God for His gifts.

There are many different types of gifts from God. Some are spiritual like mercy, grace, peace, and love. Others are physical like a home, car, and clothing. Family, good health, and financial security, also come to mind. Whatever gifts you have received in your life, make a list and tell God how much you appreciate the gifts He has given to you.

Also today, remember the gifts that you have given to others through your whisperings this year. What gifts brought the most joy to the recipients? Which whispers had the most impact in their lives? What whispers provided you the most delight? Which whispers were the most uncomfortable yet rewarding to share?

Our gives from God are boundless, just like our ability to continue to give to others.

December 2

Tell your spouse all the things they have given you emotionally, spiritually, and financially during your marriage.

Your spouse has given you a wide variety of gifts. Make a list of each and every type of gift. Make this list not only to share with your spouse but also to remind yourself of how generous and kind your spouse has been to you. Whether you are celebrating your first anniversary or your fiftieth, create a list that is lengthy and extraordinary.

Plan a private time to share your list with your spouse. If you have children, get a sitter for a special dinner alone. Create an atmosphere for your life partner to fully absorb how much you appreciate all that he or she has given you.

Be aware that your spouse may not be comfortable listening to this list. Not everyone enjoys being praised. Some people were raised in negative environments and did not learn how to accept praise when it is given. If this is the case, move slowly. However, do not give up! Persevere until you arrive at the end of your list. This may require some creativity, but you can do it.

December 3

The third day of the month, as has been the practice in this devotional, is for your children. It is also a continuation of yesterday.

Tell your children all of the things they have given you emotionally and spiritually throughout their lives. Make individual lists for each child. Share your list with each child in a way that you know will speak to that child's heart.

Some creative ways to share your thoughts include:

- ❖Write a letter.
- ❖Make a scrapbook including photos of events that moved your heart.
- ❖Take them to a place where special events happened.
- ❖Write a song to express your feelings.
- ❖Present a skit to your children that includes scenes of things that express the gifts they have given you.
- ❖Note your ideas here.

* *Assignment Whisper* *

December 4

"Give me a sentence about a public servant," said a teacher.

The small boy wrote: "The fireman came down the ladder pregnant."

The teacher took the lad aside to correct him. "Don't you know what pregnant means?" she asked.

"Sure," said the young boy confidently. "It means carrying a child."

Words are very important. They often mean different things to different people. People who were raised in other parts of the country learned alternative meanings to some vocabulary. Slang words mean one thing in Denver and something completely different in Detroit.

Watch your choice of words today. Are you using words that accurately express your meaning? Did you choose language that clearly convey your heart? Give the gift of clarity of expression today.

December 5

Remember a customer service representative at a store today.

Imagine being a customer service representative during the holiday shopping frenzy. People are frantically searching for that perfect gift, trying to stay within their budget, and rushing to meet the deadline of December 25th. The customer service personnel are not always perceived to be as helpful as you might want them to be.

Remember that these people are just doing their job. They do not make the store's policies. They have no control over what they are allowed to do to service you. They are on the front line, taking abuse for things that are outside of their power. They are between a rock and a hard place more often than not.

Take a few moments today to thank a customer service representative at a store that you frequent. Let them know that you understand their situation and appreciate their dedication to their job as well as the number of hours they will work this holiday season.

* Assignment Whisper *

December 6

Define the term "gift" today.
In the New Testament, "gift" is defined as:
1) a gift, present
   a) gifts offered in expression of honor
      1) of sacrifices and other gifts offered to God
      2) of money cast into the treasury for the purposes of the temple and for the support of the poor
2) the offering of a gift or of gifts

Webster defines the term this way:
   1. a notable capacity, talent, or endowment
   2.something voluntarily transferred by one person to another without compensation
   3. the act, right, or power of giving

Did you notice in the New Testament's definition there is nothing referring to the receiving of a gift? Each definition refers to giving a gift to another person or to God.
How do you define "gift" in your life?

December 7

<u>I asked God</u>
Author Unknown

I asked God to take away my habit.
God said, No.
It is not for me to take away,
but for you to give it up

I asked God to make my handicapped child whole.
God said, No.
His spirit is whole,
his body is only temporary

I asked God to grant me patience.
God said, No.
Patience is a byproduct of tribulations;
it isn't granted, it is learned.

I asked God to give me happiness.
God said, No.
I give you blessings;
Happiness is up to you.

I asked God to spare me pain.
God said, No.
Suffering draws you apart from worldly cares.
and brings you closer to me.

I asked God to make my spirit grow.
God said, No.
You must grow on your own!
but I will prune you to make you fruitful.

* *Assignment Whisper* *

I asked God for all things that I might enjoy life.
God said, No.
I will give you life, so that you may enjoy all things.

I asked God to help me LOVE others,
as much as He loves me.
God said...Ahhhh, finally you have the idea.

* *Assignment Whisper* *

December 8

Volunteer to help someone address their Christmas cards today.

As we age, some tasks become harder and harder. While the mind remains sharp, bodies fail faster than we would like. Fine motor skills, like handwriting, become difficult well before we are ready to stop writing.

Volunteer your hands today to help someone who can no longer write. Visit a relative, neighbor, or resident of a nursing home and address their Christmas cards. Help your friend from January 22's whispering. Think what a gift it would be to help these people stay connected with their loved ones and friends this holiday season. Imagine what joy you could bring to their lives by offering your hands for this simple task.

If no one comes to mind to help, visit your local assisted living center or nursing home. If your children are old enough, they can join the fun as well. Younger kids can lick envelops and apply stamps. The whole family can sing Christmas carols while you address envelops.

Make a family day of your visit and enjoy the whisper of serving others.

* *Assignment Whisper* *

December 9

Adopt a family for Christmas.

Contact your church or local community center to find a family in need. If you have a Christian radio station in your area, they may also be able to connect you with a family. Some agencies will collect goods and distribute them. Others will ask families for specific sizes, needs, and wishes.

This year I encourage you to select a specific family with specific needs. This may cost you more money than offering what you have in abundance. If you are financially able, select a family and meet their explicit needs. Some of these children have never received a gift in their entire lives.

Spread the news of God's love this Christmas season. Show a needy family that God's people are paying attention and expressing God's love through ordinary people. Include a Bible in your gift package to the family. Help them to learn more about God's grace.

But let all who take refuge in you be glad; let them ever sing for joy. Spread your protection over them, that those who love your name may rejoice in you.

Psalm 5:11

* *Assignment Whisper* *

December 10

"We are what we repeatedly do.
Excellence, therefore, is not an act but a habit."
Aristotle

"We judge ourselves by our intentions.
We judge others by their actions."
Ian Percy

"We judge ourselves by what we feel capable of
doing, while others judge us by what we have
already done."
Henry Wadsworth Longfellow

For in the same way you judge others, you will be judged, and with the measure you use, it will be measured to you.

Matthew 7:2

How do you judge others? How do you judge yourself? Do you judge those closest to you more harshly or more leniently than strangers? Are your expectations unrealistic?

Today, give the gift of forbearance.

December 11

Do something cheerful for a neighbor today. Are there any neighbors you have yet to meet this year? Are there neighbors that you have met that have spoken to your heart as needing more "whispers" than others? Does your neighborhood include people who are lonely and isolated from their families?

Bake a batch of cookies today and visit your new friends in your neighborhood. Let the neighbors know that you did not just visit them one time. Demonstrate that you are interested in being their friend for many years to come.

Start a new tradition in your neighborhood by hosting a cookie walk. Invite all of your neighbors to your home to enjoy some cookies. Guests bring 2-3 dozen cookies and an empty container. Each person fills their container with a variety of cookies. Each guest arrives with 2-3 dozen of the same cookies and leaves with 2-3 dozen of a variety of cookies. Of course, you can sample them throughout the evening, too! Taste testing is half the fun; the other half is meeting new friends.

Yes, I realize that December's schedule can become crazy in a big hurry. Use your cookie walk party to slow down the holiday frenzy and enjoy your friends and family. Despite the supply of cookies, do not forget the birthday cake for baby Jesus.

December 12

Call any mail order catalog ordering department today and say something encouraging to the representative who answers the phone.

Many companies hire temporary holiday staff to assist with the increased volume of orders. Even with this extra help, ordering center call lines can still be overwhelming and hectic. The people answering the phones are most likely thinking about all of the tasks yet to do to prepare their own family for their Christmas celebration.

Dial the ordering department of any mail order catalog that you receive this month. Thank the person who answers for doing their job. Spend a few minutes on the phone with them building them up and giving them a brief rest from the pace of their day. Give them the gift of God's joy over the phone. You could even sing a Christmas carol with them to make them smile.

During the rest of the year, remember those who work the ordering phone lines for a living. When you dial these numbers, make sure that you leave the representative feeling happy and relaxed after taking your order.

December 13

Mark your calendar today to spend time alone with your spouse and children during the holidays.

Christmas is normally a time for family and friends. Mothers want all of their children home for the holidays. Grandparents enjoy watching their grandchildren open their gifts. People travel many miles to gather with their family at this time of year. Time is stretched about as thin as it can go during December.

Plan now to ensure that you and your immediate family have some quality time together between now and the end of the year. Mark it on your spouse's calendar today. Text your children to make sure it is on their electronic calendars (or whatever it is kids do these days.) Get everyone committed to a specific block of time that is just for your family.

When your extended family members try to claim this time, stand firm. There are plenty of days to see the rest of the family. Plan a Christmas party for January if necessary. Explain to your extended family that it is important to you to have this time for your immediate family to celebrate together.

Make this family Christmas event an annual tradition. Encourage the rest of your family members to do the same.

Assignment Whisper *

December 14

The Donut
Author Unknown

There was a certain Professor of Religion named Dr. Christianson, a studious man who taught at a small college in the Western United States. Dr. Christianson taught the required survey course in Christianity at this particular institution. Every student was required to take this course his or her freshman year regardless of his or her major.

Although Dr. Christianson tried hard to communicate the essence of the gospel in his class, he found that most of his students looked upon the course as nothing but required drudgery. Despite his best efforts, most students refused to take Christianity seriously.

This year, Dr. Christianson had a special student named Steve. Steve was only a freshman, but was studying with the intent of going onto seminary for the ministry. Steve was popular, he was well liked, and he was an imposing physical specimen. He was now the starting center on the school football team, and was the best student in the professor's class.

One day, Dr. Christianson asked Steve to stay after class so he could talk with him. "How many push-ups can you do?"

Steve said, "I do about 200 every night."

"200? That's pretty good, Steve," Dr. Christianson said.

"Do you think you could do 300?"

Steve replied, "I don't know. I've never done 300 at a time."

"Do you think you could?" again asked Dr. Christianson.

"Well, I can try," said Steve.

* *Assignment Whisper* *

"Can you do 300 in sets of 10? I have a class project in mind and I need you to do about 300 push-ups in sets of ten for this to work. Can you do it? I need you to tell me you can do it," said the professor.

Steve said, "Well, I think I can. Yeah, I can do it."

Dr. Christianson said, "Good! I need you to do this on Friday. Let me explain what I have in mind."

Friday came and Steve got to class early and sat in the front of the room. When class started, the professor pulled out a big box of donuts. No these weren't the normal kinds of donuts, they were the extra fancy BIG kind, with cream centers and frosting swirls. Everyone was pretty excited it was Friday, the last class of the day, and they were going to get an early start on the weekend with a party in Dr. Christianson's class.

Dr. Christianson went to the first girl in the first row and asked, "Cynthia, do you want to have one of these donuts?"

Cynthia said, "Yes."

Dr. Christianson then turned to Steve and asked, "Steve, would you do ten push-ups so that Cynthia can have a donut?"

"Sure." Steve jumped down from his desk to do a quick ten.

Steve again sat in his desk. Dr. Christianson put a donut on Cynthia's desk.

Dr. Christianson then went to Joe, the next person, and asked, "Joe, do you want a donut?"

Joe said, "Yes!"

Dr. Christianson asked, "Steve would you do ten push-ups so Joe can have a donut?" Steve did ten push-ups, Joe got a donut. And so it went, down the first aisle, Steve did ten pushups for every person before they got their donut. And down the second aisle, till Dr. Christianson came to Scott.

* *Assignment Whisper* *

Scott was on the basketball team, and in as good condition as Steve. He was very popular and never lacking for female companionship. When the professor
asked, "Scott do you want a donut?"

Scott's reply was, "Well, can I do my own pushups?"

Dr. Christianson said, "No, Steve has to do them."

Then Scott said, "Well, I don't want one then."

Dr. Christianson shrugged and then turned to Steve and asked, "Steve, would you do ten pushups so Scott can have a donut he doesn't want?" With perfect obedience Steve started to do ten pushups.

Scott said, "HEY! I said I didn't want one!"

Dr. Christianson said, "Look, this is my classroom, my class, my desks, and these are my donuts. Just leave it on the desk if you don't want it." And he put a donut on Scott's desk.

Now by this time, Steve had begun to slow down a little. He just stayed on the floor between sets because it took too much effort to be getting up and down. You could start to see a little perspiration coming out around his brow. Dr. Christianson started down the third row. Now the students were beginning to get a little angry.

Dr. Christianson asked Jenny, "Jenny, do you want a donut?"

Sternly, Jenny said, "No."Then Dr. Christianson asked Steve, "Steve, would you do ten more Push-ups so Jenny can have a donut that she doesn't want?" Steve did ten....Jenny got a donut.

By now, a growing sense of uneasiness filled the room. The students were beginning to say "No" and there were all these uneaten donuts on the desks. Steve also had to really put forth a lot of extra effort to get these pushups done for each donut.

There began to be a small pool of sweat on the floor beneath his face, his arms and brow were beginning to get red because of the physical effort involved.

Dr. Christianson asked Robert, who was the most vocal unbeliever in the class, to watch Steve do each push up to make sure he did the full ten pushups in a set because he couldn't bear to watch all of Steve's work for all of those uneaten donuts. He sent Robert over to where Steve was so Robert could count the set and watch Steve closely. Dr. Christianson started down the fourth row.

During his class, however, some students from other classes had wandered in and sat down on the steps along the radiators that ran down the sides of the room. When the professor realized this, he did a quick count and saw that now there were 34 students in the room. He started to worry if Steve would be able to make it.

Dr. Christianson went on to the next person and the next and the next. Near the end of that row, Steve was really having a rough time. He was taking a lot more time to complete each set.

Steve asked Dr. Christianson, "Do I have to make my nose touch on each one?"

Dr. Christianson thought for a moment, "Well, they're your pushups.

You are in charge now. You can do them any way that you want." And Dr. Christianson went on.

A few moments later, Jason, a recent transfer student, came to the room and was about to come in when all the students yelled in one voice, "NO! Don't come in! Stay out!" Jason didn't know what was going on.

Steve picked up his head and said, "No, let him come."

Professor Christianson said, "You realize that if

* Assignment Whisper *

Jason comes in you will have to do ten pushups for him?"

Steve said, "Yes, let him come in. Give him a donut."

Dr. Christianson said, "Okay, Steve, I'll let you get Jason's out of the way right now. Jason, do you want a donut?"

Jason, new to the room hardly knew what was going on. "Yes," he said, "give me a donut."

"Steve, will you do ten push-ups so that Jason can have a donut?" Steve did ten pushups very slowly and with great effort. Jason, bewildered, was handed
a donut and sat down.

Dr. Christianson finished the fourth row, then started on those visitors seated by the heaters. Steve's arms were now shaking with each push-up in a struggle to lift himself against the force of gravity. Sweat was profusely dropping off of his face and, by this time, there was no sound except his heavy breathing, there was not a dry eye in the room.

The very last two students in the room were two young women, both cheerleaders, and very popular. Dr. Christianson went to Linda, the second to the last, and asked, "Linda, do you want a doughnut?"

Linda said, very sadly, "No, thank you."

Professor Christianson quietly asked, "Steve, would you do ten push-ups so that Linda can have a donut she doesn't want?" Grunting from the effort, Steve did ten very slow pushups for Linda.

Then Dr. Christianson turned to the last girl, Susan. "Susan, do you want a donut?"

Susan, with tears flowing down her face, began to cry. "Dr. Christianson, why can't I help him?"

Dr. Christianson, with tears of his own, said, "No, Steve has to do it alone, I have given him this task and he is in charge of seeing that everyone has an opportunity for a donut whether they want it or not. When I decided to have a party this last day of class, I looked at my grade book. Steve, here is the only student with a perfect grade. Everyone else has failed a test, skipped class, or offered me inferior work. Steve told me that in football practice, when a player messes up he must do push-ups. I told Steve that none of you could come to my party unless he paid the price by doing your push-ups. He and I made a deal for your sakes. Steve, would you do ten push-ups so Susan can have a donut?"

As Steve very slowly finished his last pushup, with the understanding that he had accomplished all that was required of him, having done 350 pushups, his arms buckled beneath him and he fell to the floor.

Dr. Christianson turned to the room and said. "And so it was, that our Savior, Jesus Christ, on the cross, pleaded to the Father, 'into thy hands I commend my spirit.' With the understanding that He had done everything that was required of Him, He yielded up His life. And like some of those in this room, many of us leave the gift on the desk, uneaten." Two students helped Steve up off the floor and to a seat, physically exhausted, but wearing a thin smile. "Well done, good and faithful servant," said the professor, adding "Not all sermons are preached in words."

Turning to his class the professor said, "My wish is that you might understand and fully comprehend all the riches of grace and mercy that have been given to you through the sacrifice of our Lord and Savior Jesus Christ. He spared not only His Begotten Son, but gave Him up for us all for the whole Church, now and forever. Whether or not we choose to accept His gift to us, the price has been paid. Wouldn't you be foolish and ungrateful to leave it laying on the desk?"

December 15

"There are two things to aim at in life. First to get what you want, and after that, to enjoy it."

These High, Green Hills
by Jan Karon
Page 326

Most of us thoroughly enjoy receiving gifts. The anticipation of what could be inside the package stimulates our curiosity. The thrill of ripping the paper from the box gets our blood flowing. The joy of discovery once the package is opened fills our hearts with love. Receiving and opening a gift is a mini aerobic workout!

But what follows? Gratitude is expressed. Hugs are often exchanged. The wrapping paper goes in the trash, and the gift is displayed in a prominent place. Did you remember to enjoy the present, or did you simply enjoy the process of receiving and opening the it? How does the gift make you feel a week from now or a year later? Does it still create joy in your heart?

Receiving God's blessings are often this way. We are grateful at the time but quickly forget how He answered our prayers. We pray for additional blessings as though He has never given us anything before.

Begin a journal today on the blessings and gifts that you have received. Whenever you receive an answer to pray or a material gift from someone, write it in your journal. Note the details as well as how the gift made you feel. Review your list throughout the year to appreciate the many gifts you have received in your life.

December 16

Volunteer with the World Youth Foundation today.

According to their website, "The World Youth Foundation (WYF) ...is an international non-governmental organization which was launched in 1994 with the aim to promote research, development and documentation of youth programmes beneficial to youths worldwide."

Their aim is, "To promote research, development and documentation of youth programmes beneficial to youth worldwide."

For those readers who are not living in the United Sates, this agency can help you find volunteer opportunities in your part of the world.

Visit their website at www.wyf.org.my for more information.

* *Assignment Whisper* *

December 17

Has this year inspired you and motivated you to do things that you never dreamed you would be doing? I certainly hope so! Please take a moment to email me about the whispering you have done this year. What fun it would be to have your accounts of the year on our website for others to read and enjoy. Let your stories inspire others to find their gift of whisper.

If you have a cause that you would like to promote or advertise, visit www.yourcause.com to register your ideas here. This website allows you to tell others about your passion without the need to create your own website.

Spend some time on this site seeing what other people are doing as well. You may find others who share your passion on other parts of the country.

December 18

<u>Twas the night Jesus came!</u>
by Audry Patricia Woolverton

'Twas the night Jesus came
and all through the house,
not a person was praying,
not one in the house..

The Bible was left
on the shelf without care,
for no one thought
Jesus would come there..

The children were dressing
to crawl into bed,
not once ever kneeling
or bowing their head..

And Mom in the rocking chair
with babe on her lap,
was watching the Late Show
as I took a nap..

When out of the east
there rose such a clatter,
I sprang to my feet
to see what was the matter.

Away to the window
I flew like a flash,
tore open the shutters
and lifted the sash.

* *Assignment Whisper* *

When what to my wondering
eyes should appear,
but Angels proclaiming
that Jesus was here.

The light of His face
made me cover my head...
was Jesus returning
just like He'd said..

And though I possessed
worldly wisdom and wealth,
I cried when I saw Him
in spite of myself..

In the Book of Life
which he held in his hand,
was written the name
of every saved man..

He spoke not a word
as he searched for my name,
when He said "it's not here"
My head hung in shame..

The people whose names
had been written with love,
He gathered to take
to his Father above..

With those who were ready
He rose without sound,
while all of the others
were left standing around...

* *Assignment Whisper* *

I fell to my knees
but it was too late,
I'd waited too long
and thus sealed my fate.

I stood and I cried
as they rose out of sight,
Oh, if only I'd known
that this was the night....

In the words of this poem
the meaning is clear
the coming of Jesus
is now drawing near...

There's only one life
and when comes the last call,
We'll find out that the Bible
was true after all...

December 19

Do something for yourself before the holiday frenzy begins in earnest. Whatever it is that calms your soul and soothes your brain, put aside some time today to do that.

Making Christmas special for your family is important to most people. People of all ages anticipate the heart-felt joy created by reuniting with family and friends. It is much easier to relax and enjoy this time together if your head and heart are at peace.

Find a couple of hours today to turn off your brain and relax your body. Turn off all electronic devises. Refuse to think about the list of things still to do. Put the worries of the world far away from you. Hand everything over to God for His safe keeping and relax.

Put your family on notice that you are going to have some time alone. Ask your spouse for some solitude. Put the dog outside. Find that one thing that can soothe your nerves and do it today. Everyone will be glad that you did, because when momma ain't happy........

December 20

Sing Christmas carols all day today. It does not matter if you cannot carry a tune. When there is a smile in your heart, your cheerfulness overpowers the flats and sharps in your voice.

Sing Christmas carols to center your heart on the true meaning of the season. Sing in public places you visit today to spread the Gospel message to those around you. Count how many people you see smiling because of your vocal praises.

If you enjoy singing Scripture, visit this website: www.blueletterbible.org. When you use this site to search on a particular verse, it will direct you to links for songs using that same verse.

The word "sing" is used 121 times in the NIV version of the Bible. If God mentioned it that many times, He must surely want us to sing praises to Him every chance that we get. Here are a few.

Sing to him, sing praise to him; tell of all his wonderful acts.

I Chronicles 16:9

I will be glad and rejoice in you; I will sing praise to your name, O Most High.

Psalm 9:2

Sing joyfully to the Lord, you righteous; it is fitting for the upright to praise him.

Psalm 33:1

I will sing to the Lord all my life; I will sing praise to my God as long as I live.

Psalm 104:33

* *Assignment Whisper* *

December 21

Thank a turkey farmer today.

The average American eats an estimated 13.7 pounds of turkey each year, and there are approximately 250 million turkeys raised in America each year. Imagine the panic across America if there were no turkeys in November and December!

Turkey farmers are can be found across the United States. If you live close to one, you might want to arrange for tour. If that is not an option, take a virtual tour by visiting this website:
www.norbest.com/virtual_turkey_tour.aspx

Although there is no mention in historical documents that turkey was served at the first Thanksgiving day in 1621, it has become part of the American tradition. Show your appreciation to the farmers who make that possible.

Here are some websites to assist you in finding a farmer to thank:

❖ www.minnesotaturkeys.com
❖ www.organic-europe.net/country_reports
❖ www.norbest.com
❖ www.sonrisefarms.net
❖ www.turkeyfed.org

December 22

Read the label on the can of cranberry sauce and give it some serious thought.

I have nothing against cranberry sauce. You will find it on our table for every Thanksgiving and Christmas feast. Yet sometimes I wonder what I am putting in my body. Chocolate is organic in a sense, but that does not necessarily mean it is healthy for my body (or so they say!)

As the new year approaches, and with it the idea of resolutions, most Americans begin to pay closer attention to what they are eating. We plan Christmas dinners, purchase extra food for holiday house guests, make shopping lists, and spend more time pushing the grocery store shopping cart than any other time of the year.

Take a moment today to read labels as you cook. Give some thought about each ingredient and how it came to be. Remember the farmers, truck drivers, dock workers, and packaging plant employees involved in putting that food on your table. Include all of those people in your prayers today. It took an incredible number of people, plants, and animals to make your Christmas feast what it is. Express your gratitude for these gifts.

December 23

After reading labels yesterday, you may be wondering about your Christmas menu today. Find a new recipe for Christmas dinner. Surprise your family by breaking out of the routine just a tad.

Set the stage for trying new things every once in awhile. Traditions are wonderful and comforting. Everyone has their favor dish that they look forward to eating on Christmas. However, new things do not replace tradition.

Perhaps you have an old family recipe that you always considered too challenging, or maybe a particular recipe is only enjoyed by one family member so you do not take the time to include it in your menu. If you are having a new addition to the family this year (through marriage, adoption, etc) try to include a new recipe that will make that person feel welcome.

Is your Christmas feast filled with traditions or habits? Do something this year to create a new tradition. Give the gift of variety to your family.

* *Assignment Whisper* *

December 24

The Christmas Rifle
Author Unknown

Pa never had much compassion for the lazy or those who squandered their means and then never had enough for the necessities. But for those who were genuinely in need, his heart was as big as all outdoors. It was from him that I learned the greatest joy in life comes from giving, not from receiving.

It was Christmas Eve 1881. I was fifteen years old and feeling like the world had caved in on me because there just hadn't been enough money to buy me the rifle that I'd wanted for Christmas. We did the chores early that night for some reason. I just figured Pa wanted a little extra time so we could read in the Bible.

After supper was over I took my boots off and stretched out in front of the fireplace and waited for Pa to get down the old Bible. I was still feeling sorry for myself and, to be honest, I wasn't in much of a mood to read Scriptures. But Pa didn't get the Bible, instead he bundled up again and went outside. I couldn't figure it out because we had already done all the chores. I didn't worry about it long though, I was too busy wallowing in self-pity.

Soon Pa came back in. It was a cold clear night out and there was ice in his beard.

"Come on, Matt," he said. "Bundle up good, it's cold out tonight."

I was really upset then. Not only wasn't I getting the rifle for Christmas, now Pa was dragging me out in the cold, and for no earthly reason that I could see. We'd already done all the chores, and I couldn't think of anything else that needed doing, especially not on a night like this.

But I knew Pa was not very patient at one dragging one's feet when he'd told them to do something, so I got up and put my boots back on and got my cap, coat, and mittens. Ma gave me a mysterious smile as I opened the door to leave the house. Something was up, but I didn't know what.

Outside, I became even more dismayed. There in front of the house was the work team, already hitched to the big sled. Whatever it was we were going to do wasn't going to be a short, quick, little job. I could tell. We never hitched up this sled unless we were going to haul a big load.

Pa was already up on the seat, reins in hand. I reluctantly climbed up beside him. The cold was already biting at me. I wasn't happy. When I was on, Pa pulled the sled around the house and stopped in front of the woodshed. He got off and I followed.

"I think we'll put on the high sideboards," he said. "Here, help me."

The high sideboards! It had been a bigger job than I wanted to do with just the low sideboards on, but whatever it was we were going to do would be a lot bigger with the high side boards on.

After we had exchanged the sideboards, Pa went into the woodshed and came out with an armload of wood - the wood I'd spent all summer hauling down from the mountain, and then all Fall sawing into block and splitting. What was he doing? Finally I said something.

"Pa," I asked, "what are you doing?"

"You been by the Widow Jensen's lately?" he asked.

The Widow Jensen lived about two miles down the road. Her husband had died a year or so before and left her with three children, the oldest being eight. Sure, I'd been by, but so what?

"Yeah," I said, "Why?"

"I rode by just today," Pa said. "Little Jakey was out digging around in the woodpile trying to find a few chips. They're out of wood, Matt."

That was all he said and then he turned and went back into the woodshed for another armload of wood.

I followed him. We loaded the sled so high that I began to wonder if the horses would be able to pull it. Finally, Pa called a halt to our loading, then we went to the smoke house and Pa took down a big ham and a side of bacon. He handed them to me and told me to put them in the sled and wait. When he returned he was carrying a sack of flour over his right shoulder and a smaller sack of something in his left hand.

"What's in the little sack?" I asked.

"Shoes, they're out of shoes. Little Jakey just had gunny sacks wrapped around his feet when he was out in the woodpile this morning. I got the children a little candy too. It just wouldn't be Christmas without a little candy."

We rode the two miles to Widow Jensen's pretty much in silence. I tried to think through what Pa was doing. We didn't have much by worldly standards. Of course, we did have a big woodpile, though most of what was left now was still in the form of logs that I would have to saw into blocks and split before we could use it. We also had meat and flour, so we could spare that, but I knew we didn't have any money, so why was Pa buying them shoes and candy? Really, why was he doing any of this? Widow Jensen had closer neighbors than us; it shouldn't have been our concern.

We came in from the blind side of the Jensen house and unloaded the wood as quietly as possible, then we took the meat and flour and shoes to the door. We knocked.

The door opened a crack and a timid voice said, "Who is it?"

"Lucas Miles, Ma'am, and my son, Matt, could we come in for a bit?"

Widow Jensen opened the door and let us in. She had a blanket wrapped around her shoulders. The children were wrapped in another and were sitting in front of the fireplace by a very small fire that hardly gave off any heat at all. Widow Jensen fumbled with a match and finally lit the lamp.

"We brought you a few things, Ma'am," Pa said and set down the sack of flour.

I put the meat on the table. Then Pa handed her the sack that had the shoes in it. She opened it hesitantly and took the shoes out one pair at a time. There was a pair for her and one for each of the children - sturdy shoes, the best, shoes that would last. I watched her carefully. She bit her lower lip to keep it from trembling and then tears filled her eyes and started running down her cheeks. She looked up at Pa like she wanted to say something, but it wouldn't come out.

"We brought a load of wood too, Ma'am," Pa said.

He turned to me and said, "Matt, go bring in enough to last awhile. Let's get that fire up to size and heat this place up."

I wasn't the same person when I went back out to bring in the wood. I had a big lump in my throat and as much as I hate to admit it, there were tears in my eyes too. In my mind I kept seeing those three kids huddled around the fireplace and their mother standing there with tears running down her cheeks with so much gratitude in her heart that she couldn't speak.

My heart swelled within me and a joy that I'd never known before, filled my soul. I had given at Christmas many times before, but never when it had made so much difference. I could see we were literally saving the lives of these people.

I soon had the fire blazing and everyone's spirits soared. The kids started giggling when Pa handed them each a piece of candy and Widow Jensen looked on with a smile that probably hadn't crossed her face for a long time. She finally turned to us.

"God bless you," she said. "I know the Lord has sent you. The children and I have been praying that he would send one of his angels to spare us."

In spite of myself, the lump returned to my throat and the tears welled up in my eyes again. I'd never thought of Pa in those exact terms before, but after Widow Jensen mentioned it I could see that it was probably true. I was sure that a better man than Pa had never walked the earth. I started remembering all the times he had gone out of his way for Ma and me, and many others. The list seemed endless as I thought on it.

Pa insisted that everyone try on the shoes before we left. I was amazed when they all fit and I wondered how he had known what sizes to get. Then I guessed that if he was on an errand for the Lord that the Lord would make sure he got the right sizes.

Tears were running down Widow Jensen's face again when we stood up to leave. Pa took each of the kids in his big arms and gave them a hug. They clung to him and didn't want us to go. I could see that they missed their Pa, and I was glad that I still had mine.

At the door Pa turned to Widow Jensen and said, "The Mrs. wanted me to invite you and the children over for Christmas dinner tomorrow. The turkey will be more than the three of us can eat, and a man can get cantankerous if he has to eat turkey for too many meals. We'll be by to get you about eleven. It'll be nice to have some little ones around again. Matt, here, hasn't been little for quite a spell."

I was the youngest. My two brothers and two sisters had all married and had moved away.

Widow Jensen nodded and said, "Thank you, Brother Miles. I don't have to say, May the Lord bless you, I know for certain that He will."

Out on the sled I felt a warmth that came from deep within and I didn't even notice the cold.

When we had gone a ways, Pa turned to me and said, "Matt, I want you to know something. Your ma and me have been tucking a little money away here and there all year so we could buy that rifle for you, but we didn't have quite enough. Then yesterday a man who owed me a little money from years back came by to make things square. Your ma and me were real excited, thinking that now we could get you that rifle, and I started into town this morning to do just that, but on the way I saw little Jakey out scratching in the woodpile with his feet wrapped in those gunny sacks and I knew what I had to do. Son, I spent the money for shoes and a little candy for those children. I hope you understand."

I understood, and my eyes became wet with tears again. I understood very well, and I was so glad Pa had done it. Now the rifle seemed very low on my list of priorities. Pa had given me a lot more. He had given me the look on Widow Jensen's face and the radiant smiles of her three children.

For the rest of my life, whenever I saw any of the Jensens, or split a block of wood, I remembered, and remembering brought back that same joy I felt riding home beside Pa that night. Pa had given me much more than a rifle that night, he had given me the best Christmas of my life.

Assignment Whisper *

December 25

Nativity Story
Author unknown

There was once a man who didn't believe in God, and he didn't hesitate to let others know how he felt about religion and religious holidays, like Christmas. His wife, however, did believe, and she raised their children to also have faith in God and Jesus, despite his disparaging comments.

One snowy Christmas Eve, his wife was taking their children to a Christmas Eve service in the farm community in which they lived. She asked him to come, but he refused.

"That story is nonsense!" he said. "Why would God lower Himself to come to Earth as a man? That's ridiculous!" So she and the children left, and he stayed home.

A while later, the winds grew stronger and the snow turned into a blizzard. As the man looked out the window, all he saw was a blinding snowstorm. He sat down to relax before the fire for the evening. Then he heard a loud thump. Something had hit the window. Then another thump. He looked out, but couldn't see more than a few feet.

When the snow let up a little, he ventured outside to see what could have been beating on his window. In the field near his house he saw a flock of wild geese.

Apparently they had been flying south for the winter when they got caught in the snowstorm and couldn't go on. They were lost and stranded on his farm, with no food or shelter. They just flapped their wings and flew around the field in low circles, blindly and aimlessly. A couple of them had flown into his window, it seemed.

* *Assignment Whisper* *

The man felt sorry for the geese and wanted to help them. The barn would be a great place for them to stay, he thought. It's warm and safe; surely they could spend the night and wait out the storm. So he walked over to the barn and opened the doors wide, then watched and waited, hoping they would notice the open barn and go inside. But the geese just fluttered around aimlessly and didn't seem to notice the barn or realize what it could mean for them.

The man tried to get their attention, but that just seemed to scare them and they moved further away. He went into the house and came with some bread, broke it up, and made a breadcrumb trail leading to the barn. They still didn't catch on. Now he was getting frustrated. He got behind them and tried to shoo them toward the barn, but they only got more scared and scattered in every direction except toward the barn. Nothing he did could get them to go into the barn where they would be warm and safe.

"Why don't they follow me?!" he exclaimed. "Can't they see this is the only place where they can survive the storm?"

He thought for a moment and realized that they just wouldn't follow a human. "If only I were a goose, then I could save them," he said out loud.

Then he had an idea. He went into barn, got one of his own geese, and carried it in his arms as he circled around behind the flock of wild geese. He then released it. His goose flew through the flock and straight into the barn-and one by one the other geese followed it to safety.

He stood silently for a moment as the words he had spoken a few minutes earlier replayed in his mind: If only I were a goose, then I could save them!"

Then he thought about what he had said to his wife earlier. "Why would God want to be like us? That's ridiculous!" Suddenly it all made sense. That is what God had done. We were like the geese-blind, lost, perishing. God had His Son become like us so He could show us the way and save us. That was the meaning of Christmas, he realized.

As the winds and blinding snow died down, his soul became quiet and pondered this wonderful thought. Suddenly he understood what Christmas was all about, why Christ had come. Years of doubt and disbelief vanished like the passing storm. He fell to his knees in the snow, and prayed his first prayer: "Thank You, God, for coming in human form to get me out of the storm!"

* *Assignment Whisper* *

December 26

Deliver a plate of leftovers to a shut-in today.

Some people really love cold turkey sandwiches and seldom have the opportunity to enjoy them. Other people enjoyed Christmas day at someone else's home and returned home to an empty freezer. Many people just plain like leftovers.

If you volunteered for Meals on Wheels this Christmas season, perhaps you already know someone who could use a meal today. Maybe you met a neighbor this year whom you know will be alone today, or visit that sibling who was not able to attend the family affair yesterday. They would probably enjoy the fellowship as much as the food.

Take your family with you. Now that you learned new Christmas carols on December 20's whispering, you can sing songs together, too.

December 27

Donate your left over Christmas cards and wrapping paper to a nursing home, hospice, or hospital for next year.

Each year I deliberately put my left over Christmas cards in a "safe" place so that they will be readily available next December when I am ready to send out my cards. I do not store them with Christmas decorations. By the time I dig out the decorations, it would be too late for cards. It would be better to store Valentine Cards in my Christmas decorations. Such are my organizational skills! Yet I routinely forget where that "safe" place is from year to year, and off I go to buy more.

Instead of putting your surplus of cards in that "safe" place this year, donate them now to someone who can use them next year. They will go to much better use this way and will not clutter your house until then.

If you have extra wrapping paper, donate that as well. Nursing homes and hospitals can use it to decorate next year.

* *Assignment Whisper* *

December 28

Better is the end of a thing than the beginning thereof.

Ecclesiastes 7:8

Look at David's Lord and Master; see His beginning. He was despised and rejected of men; a man of sorrows and acquainted with grief. Would you see the end? He sits at His Father's right hand, expecting until His enemies be made his footstool. "As He is, so are we also in this world." You must bear the cross, or you shall never wear the crown; you must wade through the mire, or you shall never walk the golden pavement. Cheer up, then, poor Christian. "Better is the end of a thing than the beginning thereof." See that creeping worm, how contemptible its appearance! It is the beginning of a thing. Mark that insect with gorgeous wings, playing in the sunbeams, sipping at the flower bells, full of happiness and life; that is the end thereof. That caterpillar is yourself, until you are wrapped up in the chrysalis of death; but when Christ shall appear you shall be like Him, for you shall see Him as He is. Be content to be like Him, a worm and no man, that like Him you may be satisfied when you wake up in His likeness. That rough-looking diamond is put upon the wheel of the lapidary. He cuts it on all sides. It loses much--much that seemed costly to itself. The king is crowned; the diadem is put upon the monarch's head with trumpet's joyful sound. A glittering ray flashes from that coronet, and it beams from that very diamond which was just now so sorely vexed by the lapidary. You may venture to compare yourself to such a diamond, for you are one of God's people; and this is the time of the cutting process. Let faith and patience have their perfect work, for in the day when the crown shall be set upon the head of the King, Eternal, Immortal, Invisible, one ray of glory shall stream from you. "They shall be Mine," saith the Lord, "in the day when I make up My jewels." "Better is the end of a thing than the beginning thereof."

by C. H. Spurgeon

December 29

Make a list of the whispering that you did this year that really made a difference in your life. Review the notes that you made to remind yourself of the fun you had.

Consider these questions:

❖What moved you the most?

❖Which whispers surprised you the most?

❖What days did you regret skipping?

❖Which whispers brought the most joy to the recipients?

❖When did whispering begin to feel natural to you?

❖How did your spouse respond to your whispers?

❖How has your family changed because of whispering together?

Make a plan for what you will continue to do in the coming year. Which whispers will you try next year that you skipped this year? What friends will you share the devotional with next year?

Assignment Whisper *

December 30

Here is one last volunteering resource for those of you who are either still looking for ideas or procrastinated until the last moment. Yes, I know some of you had good intentions on January 1st. It is never too late.

Visit this website to find opportunities in your area: www.volunteermatch.org.

* *Assignment Whisper* *

December 31

Today is a day of celebration. Let the fireworks begin. Throw confetti in the air. Feel the festive atmosphere down to your toes.

While I am not encouraging prideful or arrogant behavior, celebrate the joy that you found in whispering today. Give yourself a pat on the back for all that you did and all that you gained from serving others. Be proud in a humble way.

I am celebrating that you persevered to the end. Log on to the *Assignment Whisper* website (www.assignmentwhisper.com) today to read what others have done during the year and share in their joy and accomplishments. Together, we can change the world, one whisper at a time.

Celebrate the joy of whispering, today and every day.

Notes

* *Assignment Whisper* *

Notes

* *Assignment Whisper* *

Ordering Information

To order your copy of *Assignment Whisper,* please visit www.lulu.com. Remember to order one for a friend, too. Profits from book sales are used for *Assignment Whisper* charity events.

Read information regarding other *Assignment Whisper* events and ideas on my website www.assignmentwhisper.com today. Email your ideas and whispering experiences for everyone to read.

* Assignment Whisper *

www.ingramcontent.com/pod-product-compliance
Lightning Source LLC
Chambersburg PA
CBHW020601270326
41927CB00005B/120